fresh and simple™

vegetable dinners

BARNES
& NOBLE
BOOKS
NEW YORK

Pictured on front cover:

Sweet & Spicy Spring Rolls, *page 83*

Pictured on title page:

Cavatelli with Arugula & Dried Cranberries, *page 30*

Previously published as
Better Homes and Gardens® Fresh and Simple™ Vegetable Dinners

Copyright © 2004, 1999 by Meredith Corporation, Des Moines, Iowa. First Edition.

This edition published for Barnes & Noble, Inc., by Meredith Books.

Printed in China

ISBN: 0-7607-6025-X

contents

why not vegetables for a change!

Move over meat. Vegetables are the new main course, along with their savory sidekicks—protein-powerful beans and grains, the elegant egg, and everyone's favorite, pasta. The goal today? Eat fresh, stay healthy. That means fresh vegetables in abundance and meat on the side (or even skipped altogether—it's up to you). *Vegetable Dinners*, inspired by the ever-growing bounty at produce counters, offers myriad ways to energize mealtime with vegetable power. The 64 quick and simple recipes serve up proof that good taste knows no season.

bravo!
beans
&grains

corn waffles with tomato salsa

Morning to night, waffles have timeless appeal. For a simple supper, try this twist on tacos—stud waffles with kernels of corn and top them with a lively black bean salsa. A cornmeal mix streamlines preparation.

Start to finish: 30 minutes Makes 4 servings

For salsa, brush tomato halves with 1 teaspoon of the olive oil; place on the unheated rack of a broiler pan. Broil 4 to 5 inches from the heat for 8 to 10 minutes or until tomatoes begin to char, turning once. Remove from broiler pan and cool slightly; coarsely chop.

Meanwhile, in a medium bowl combine the remaining 1 teaspoon olive oil, beans, green onions, cilantro, lime juice, serrano pepper, and salt. Stir in tomatoes and any juices. Set aside.

For waffles, prepare corn muffin mix according to package directions, except stir corn into batter. (If necessary, add 1 to 2 additional tablespoons milk to thin batter.)

Pour about half of the batter onto the grid of a preheated, lightly greased waffle baker. Close lid quickly; do not open until done. Bake according to manufacturer's directions. When done, use a fork to lift waffle off grid; keep warm. Repeat with remaining batter.

To serve, cut waffles in half. Divide warm waffles among 4 serving plates. Dollop with salsa and yogurt. If desired, garnish with cilantro.

Nutrition facts per serving: 417 cal., 12 g total fat (3 g sat. fat), 55 mg chol., 841 mg sodium, 70 g carbo., 8 g fiber, 15 g pro. Daily values: 14% vit. A, 46% vit. C, 12% calcium, 21% iron

- 6 plum tomatoes, halved
- 2 teaspoons olive oil
- 1 15-ounce can black beans or small white beans, rinsed and drained
- ⅓ cup sliced green onions
- 2 tablespoons snipped fresh cilantro or parsley
- 2 tablespoons lime juice
- 1 to 2 serrano peppers, chopped
- ¼ teaspoon salt
- 1 8½-ounce package corn muffin mix
- ½ cup fresh or frozen whole kernel corn
- ¼ cup plain fat-free yogurt
- Fresh cilantro sprigs (optional)

toasted barley with
baked goat cheese

Softened by heat, baked goat cheese cloaks barley and vegetables in an irresistible sauce. Be sure to set a big spoon at each place so diners can scoop up every last bit.

8

- 1 **cup quick-cooking barley**
- 1 **14½-ounce can vegetable or chicken broth**
- 1 **medium leek or 3 green onions, sliced**
- 1 **cup frozen peas**
- 2 **tablespoons snipped fresh mint**
- 8 **ounces semisoft goat cheese (chèvre)**
- ¼ **cup fine dry bread crumbs**

Start to finish: 30 minutes   Makes 4 servings

Place barley in a large, heavy skillet. Cook over medium heat about 10 minutes or until lightly toasted, stirring frequently. Remove from heat. Slowly stir in broth and leek; return to heat. Bring to boiling. Reduce heat; simmer, covered, 10 to 12 minutes or until barley is tender and liquid is absorbed. Stir in peas and mint; heat through.

Meanwhile, shape goat cheese into 8 balls. Flatten slightly into rounds about 1½ inches in diameter. Place bread crumbs in a shallow dish. Coat both sides of each cheese round with bread crumbs. Place on a baking sheet lined with foil. Bake in a 400° oven for 4 to 5 minutes or until soft and warm.

To serve, spoon the barley mixture onto 4 serving plates; top with cheese rounds.

Nutrition facts per serving: 414 cal., 18 g total fat (9 g sat. fat), 50 mg chol., 831 mg sodium, 49 g carbo., 6 g fiber, 18 g pro. Daily values: 11% vit. A, 10% vit. C, 7% calcium, 17% iron

spicy limas
with pita bread

Tossed together as a chunky topping for pita "tacos," chile peppers, lima beans, and tomatoes are hot stuff. This toothsome trio may seem ultramodern, but its goodness is time-tested—all three grew here long before the Mayflower arrived.

Start to finish: 25 minutes   **Makes 4 servings**

Cook lima beans according to package directions; drain and return to saucepan. Stir in jalapeño peppers, tomatoes, cilantro, and salt; toss until combined.

Meanwhile, place pita rounds in a single layer on a large baking sheet. Spray pitas lightly with nonstick coating; sprinkle lightly with garlic salt. Bake in a 350° oven for 10 to 12 minutes or until crisp.

To serve, place a pita round on each serving plate. Spoon lima bean mixture atop. Dollop with yogurt and salsa.

Nutrition facts per serving: 389 cal., 2 g total fat (0 g sat. fat), 1 mg chol., 562 mg sodium, 74 g carbo., 6 g fiber, 20 g pro. Daily values: 6% vit. A, 36% vit. C, 9% calcium, 40% iron

- 1   **10-ounce package frozen baby lima beans**
- 2   **jalapeño or serrano peppers, seeded and chopped, or ⅛ to ¼ teaspoon crushed red pepper**
- 2   **medium tomatoes, seeded and chopped, or 4 plum tomatoes, chopped**
- 2   **tablespoons snipped fresh cilantro**
- ¼   **teaspoon salt**
- 4   **pita bread rounds**
-    **Nonstick spray coating**
-    **Garlic salt**
- ¼   **cup plain low-fat yogurt**
- ¼   **cup salsa**

fire alarm

All chili peppers have five-alarm oils in their flesh and seeds that can burn your eyes and lips. Wash your hands well after handling chilis and don't touch anything until you do. Better still, before you start, cover your hands with plastic bags or disposable gloves. Because these oils transfer to knives and cutting surfaces, wash tools thoroughly after using so the oils won't transfer to other foods.

spaghetti squash with balsamic beans

It's not magic, just Mother Nature. When cooked, the golden flesh of spaghetti squash separates into strands that look like the ever popular pasta. Top the squash strands with this sassy sauce of sweet-tart beans.

1 medium spaghetti squash (2½ to 3 pounds), halved and seeded

1 10-ounce package frozen baby lima beans

1 15-ounce can red kidney beans, rinsed and drained

½ of a 7-ounce jar (½ cup) roasted red sweet peppers, rinsed, drained, and cut into short strips

½ teaspoon salt

¼ cup balsamic vinegar

3 tablespoons olive oil

1 tablespoon honey mustard

2 cloves garlic, minced

Start to finish: 30 minutes   Makes 4 servings

Place squash halves in a large Dutch oven with about 1 inch of water. Bring to boiling. Cook, covered, for 15 to 20 minutes or until tender.

Meanwhile, in a saucepan cook lima beans according to package directions, adding kidney beans during the last 3 minutes of cooking; drain and return to pan. Stir in roasted red peppers and salt; heat through.

Meanwhile, for vinaigrette,* in a screw-top jar combine vinegar, oil, honey mustard, and garlic. Cover and shake well. Pour over warm bean mixture; toss to coat.

Use a fork to scrape the squash pulp from the shells in strands; return strands to each shell. Spoon warm bean mixture atop squash strands in shells, drizzling any excess vinaigrette on top. If desired, sprinkle with freshly ground pepper. To serve, cut each squash shell in half.

Nutrition facts per serving: 421 cal., 11 g total fat (2 g sat. fat), 0 mg chol., 466 mg sodium, 65 g carbo., 13 g fiber, 21 g pro. Daily values: 9% vit. A, 94% vit. C, 6% calcium, 42% iron

Note: The vinaigrette may be prepared ahead and refrigerated for up to 2 days. Allow it to sit at room temperature while preparing squash and beans.

cajun beans & barley

As lively as a Cajun two-step, this dish will dance to the table in record time. Quick-cooking barley and canned pinto beans, freshened with a trio of colorful vegetables, ready this meal in minutes.

¾ cup water

½ cup quick-cooking barley

¼ cup chopped onion

1 15-ounce can pinto beans,
    rinsed and drained

1 14½-ounce can stewed
    tomatoes, undrained

1 cup frozen whole kernel corn

¼ cup chopped green sweet pepper

1 teaspoon Cajun seasoning or
    ½ teaspoon crushed red pepper

4 ¾-inch-thick slices French
    bread, toasted, or 4 rusks

Start to finish: 15 minutes   Makes 4 servings

In a medium saucepan bring water to boiling. Stir in barley and onion. Return to boiling. Reduce heat and simmer, covered, 10 to 12 minutes or until barley is tender and water is absorbed.

Stir pinto beans, undrained tomatoes, corn, sweet pepper, and Cajun seasoning into barley mixture. Cook, covered, over medium heat until bubbly. Cook, covered, for 2 to 3 minutes more or until corn is tender. Serve over toasted French bread.

Nutrition facts per serving: 306 cal., 2 g total fat (0 g sat. fat), 0 mg chol., 962 mg sodium, 63 g carbo., 8 g fiber, 12 g pro. Daily values: 6% vit. A, 23% vit. C, 6% calcium, 20% iron

bean **cuisine**

Fiber- and protein-rich dried beans now come in a dazzling array of colors and sizes, from the once-rare heirloom varieties to intriguing exotics. Home-cooked beans are as convenient as canned and better for you as they are free of preservatives and sodium. When time permits, freeze cooked beans in 2-cup portions to substitute for a 15-ounce can of beans.

polenta with mushrooms & asparagus

Something green always beats the winter blues. This rustic polenta, starring spring's first asparagus, may bring just the lift you need. A little chocolate for dessert will prolong the good mood.

Start to finish: 30 minutes   Makes 4 servings

Prepare polenta according to package directions. Cover and keep warm.

Meanwhile, in a large skillet cook onion in hot oil over medium heat until tender. Add mushrooms, asparagus, and garlic; cook, uncovered, about 4 minutes or until almost tender. Stir in wine and salt. Cook, uncovered, over medium-high heat for 1 minute.

To serve, divide polenta among 4 serving bowls. Spoon the mushroom mixture over polenta. Sprinkle with Parmesan cheese and nuts.

Nutrition facts per serving: 426 cal., 12 g total fat (1 g sat. fat), 5 mg chol., 220 mg sodium, 64 g carbo., 10 g fiber, 14 g pro. Daily values: 6% vit. A, 33% vit. C, 9% calcium, 16% iron

1 cup instant or quick-cooking polenta

1 small onion, chopped (⅓ cup)

1 tablespoon olive oil

3 cups sliced fresh mushrooms, such as cremini, shiitake, or oyster

1 pound asparagus spears, trimmed and cut into 1-inch pieces (2¼ cups)

3 cloves garlic, minced

⅓ cup dry white wine, marsala, vegetable broth, or chicken broth

¼ teaspoon salt

¼ cup finely shredded Parmesan cheese

⅓ cup chopped walnuts or pecans, or pine nuts, toasted

christmas limas with pesto bulgur

Dappled red over pale green, Christmas limas are aptly named and easy to spot, but it's their nutty flavor that makes them a standout in this Italian-inspired meal. Cook the beans ahead or use canned beans when dinner is really last minute.

15

Start to finish: 20 minutes   Makes 6 servings

In a medium saucepan bring broth to boiling; add bulgur. Return to boiling. Reduce heat and simmer, covered, for 10 minutes. Remove from heat. Stir in sweet pepper, green onions, pesto sauce, and beans. Season with pepper. Serve with toasted bread slices.

Nutrition facts per serving: 288 cal., 11 g total fat (0 g sat. fat), 2 mg chol., 542 mg sodium, 41 g carbo., 5 g fiber, 9 g pro. Daily values: 10% vit. A, 36% vit. C, 3% calcium, 10% iron

Note: To cook beans, rinse ¾ cup dried beans and combine with 5 cups water in a large Dutch oven. Bring to boiling. Reduce heat and simmer for 2 minutes. Remove from heat. Cover and let stand for 1 hour. Drain and rinse beans. Return beans to pan. Add 5 cups fresh water. Bring to boiling. Reduce heat and simmer, covered, for 1¼ to 1½ hours or until tender; drain. (Or, place beans in 5 cups cold water in a Dutch oven. Cover and let soak in a cool place overnight.)

1⅓ cups vegetable or chicken broth

⅔ cup bulgur

1 medium red sweet pepper, chopped

¼ cup thinly sliced green onions

⅓ cup refrigerated pesto sauce

2 cups cooked Christmas lima beans, pinto beans, or cranberry beans* or one 15-ounce can pinto beans, rinsed and drained

Freshly ground pepper

Toasted bread slices

lentil & veggie tostadas

Sign up here for Dinner 101! This hearty, healthful entrée is ideal weeknight family fare and so easy that even rookie chefs can help prepare it.

Start to finish: 25 minutes   Makes 4 servings

In a medium saucepan stir together water, lentils, onion, cilantro, salt, cumin, and garlic. Bring to boiling. Reduce heat and simmer, covered, for 12 to 15 minutes or until lentils are tender and most of the liquid is absorbed. Use a fork to mash the cooked lentils.

Spread the lentil mixture on tostada shells; top with vegetables and cheese. Place on a large baking sheet. Broil 3 to 4 inches from the heat about 2 minutes or until cheese melts. Serve immediately.

Nutrition facts per serving: 288 cal., 11 g total fat (5 g sat. fat), 20 mg chol., 497 mg sodium, 34 g carbo., 7 g fiber, 16 g pro. Daily values: 24% vit. A, 68% vit. C, 18% calcium, 19% iron

1¾   cups water

¾   cup dry red lentils, rinsed
     and drained

¼   cup chopped onion

1   to 2 tablespoons snipped
     fresh cilantro

½   teaspoon salt

½   teaspoon ground cumin

1   clove garlic, minced

4   tostada shells

2   cups assorted chopped
     vegetables (such as broccoli,
     tomato, zucchini, and/or
     yellow summer squash)

¾   cup shredded Monterey Jack
     cheese (3 ounces)

garlic pilaf
with cajun eggplant

Native to the Americas, protein-packed quinoa (KEEN-wah) is an ancient grain but a recent arrival on American tables. It cooks like rice and has a mild flavor and slightly chewy texture. You'll find it at natural food stores and larger supermarkets.

18

½ cup chopped onion

1 teaspoon olive oil

6 cloves garlic, minced

2 cups water

1 cup quinoa, rinsed and drained, or long grain rice

1 cup coarsely shredded carrot

1 teaspoon Cajun seasoning

½ teaspoon salt

1 15-ounce can hominy, rinsed and drained

1 tablespoon snipped fresh basil, rosemary, chives, thyme, or oregano

1 medium eggplant, cut into ½-inch-thick slices

2 teaspoons olive oil

Cajun seasoning

Start to finish: 30 minutes   Makes 4 servings

In a medium saucepan cook the onion in the 1 teaspoon hot oil over medium heat for 3 minutes. Add garlic; cook 1 minute more. Stir in water, quinoa, carrot, 1 teaspoon Cajun seasoning, and salt.

Bring to boiling. Reduce heat and simmer, covered, about 15 minutes or until quinoa is tender and liquid is absorbed. Stir in hominy and desired herb. Cover and let stand for 1 minute.

Meanwhile, brush eggplant slices lightly with the 2 teaspoons oil; sprinkle with additional Cajun seasoning. Place on the unheated rack of a broiler pan. Broil 4 to 5 inches from the heat for 2½ to 3 minutes on each side or just until tender.

To serve, divide the eggplant slices among 4 serving plates. Top with the quinoa mixture.

Nutrition facts per serving: 296 cal., 7 g total fat (1 g sat. fat), 0 mg chol., 499 mg sodium, 52 g carbo., 7 g fiber, 8 g pro. Daily values: 87% vit. A, 7% vit. C, 5% calcium, 34% iron

greek basmati rice

Taste why fusion cooking is all the rage. This cross-cultural toss blends exotic basmati rice—favored by Indian cooks for its delicate fragrance—with essentials of the classic Greek salad.

Start to finish: 30 minutes   Makes 4 servings

In a medium saucepan bring water to boiling. Stir in rice and salt. Return to boiling. Reduce heat and simmer, covered, about 15 minutes or until rice is tender and liquid is absorbed.

Stir spinach and dill into cooked rice. Cover and let stand for 5 minutes. Stir in chopped tomato, lemon peel, and lemon juice. To serve, divide mixture among 4 servings plates. Sprinkle each serving with feta cheese.

Nutrition facts per serving: 270 cal., 7 g total fat (5 g sat. fat), 28 mg chol., 520 mg sodium, 42 g carbo., 2 g fiber, 9 g pro. Daily values: 25% vit. A, 33% vit. C, 17% calcium, 21% iron

eau de rice

Aromatic rice enhances the exotic in stir-fries, salads, stuffings, pilafs, and desserts. Use as you would long grain rice in any recipe. Basmati, a long grain brown or white rice from India and California, is nutty and fluffy. Texmati rice is a milder basmati hybrid, while wild pecan is a white rice with the aroma and flavor of its namesake. Jasmine rice is delicately floral. All are commonly available in supermarkets.

2 cups water

1 cup basmati rice or long grain rice

¼ teaspoon salt

2 cups shredded fresh spinach

1 teaspoon snipped fresh dill

1 large tomato, seeded and chopped (about ¾ cup)

1 teaspoon finely shredded lemon peel

2 tablespoons lemon juice

½ cup crumbled feta cheese (2 ounces)

broccoli rabe over polenta

Italians adore chubby broccoli's more slender cruciferous cousin, broccoli rabe (also called rapini). Here its pleasantly bitter flavor and crunchy texture contrast with the more subtle and creamy polenta.

1 **cup instant or quick-cooking polenta**

1 **cup vegetable or chicken broth**

1 **tablespoon cornstarch**

1 **cup chopped sweet onion, such as Vidalia or Walla Walla**

4 **teaspoons olive oil**

3 **cloves garlic, minced**

1 **pound broccoli rabe, coarsely chopped (about 7 cups), or 3 cups coarsely chopped broccoli flowerets**

½ **of a 7-ounce jar (½ cup) roasted red sweet peppers, rinsed, drained, and chopped**

¼ **cup pine nuts or slivered almonds, toasted**

Start to finish: 30 minutes   Makes 4 servings

Prepare polenta according to package directions. Cover and keep warm.

In a small bowl stir together broth and cornstarch. Set aside.

In a large skillet cook onion in hot oil over medium heat 4 to 5 minutes or until tender. Add garlic; cook 30 seconds more. Add broccoli rabe; cover and cook about 3 minutes or just until tender. (If using broccoli flowerets, cook and stir 3 to 4 minutes or until crisp-tender.) Stir in roasted sweet peppers.

Stir cornstarch mixture; add to vegetable mixture. Cook and stir until thickened and bubbly. Cook and stir 2 minutes more.

To serve, divide polenta among 4 serving plates. Spoon the vegetable mixture over cooked polenta. Sprinkle each serving with nuts.

Nutrition facts per serving: 394 cal., 11 g total fat (1 g sat. fat), 0 mg chol., 256 mg sodium, 67 g carbo., 11 g fiber, 12 g pro. Daily values: 21% vit. A, 194% vit. C, 5% calcium, 18% iron

buckwheat & carrots

Rice is what you'd expect here, but substitute nutty, protein-rich buckwheat groats, and it's a whole new grain game. You'll find roasted buckwheat groats sold as kasha.

1   14½-ounce can vegetable
    or chicken broth

¼   cup water

1   cup buckwheat groats or kasha

⅛   teaspoon ground nutmeg

12   ounces green beans, bias-sliced
    into 1-inch pieces (2 cups)

1   cup shredded carrots

Start to finish: 25 minutes   Makes 4 servings

In a medium saucepan bring broth and water to boiling. Stir in the buckwheat groats and nutmeg. Return to boiling. Reduce heat and simmer, covered, for 5 minutes (20 minutes for the kasha).

Add green beans; cook about 5 minutes more or until grain is tender and green beans are crisp-tender. Stir in shredded carrots. Serve warm.

Nutrition facts per serving: 183 cal., 2 g total fat (0 g sat. fat), 0 mg chol., 437 mg sodium, 42 g carbo., 6 g fiber, 7 g pro. Daily values: 83% vit. A, 17% vit. C, 4% calcium, 15% iron

wild rice quesadillas

Adding earthy flavor to a favorite fast food, wild rice shrugs off its black tie reputation and goes casual. When minutes matter, use any variety of leftover cooked rice or plan to cook the rice ahead of time.

23

Start to finish: 20 minutes   Makes 3 servings

In a medium bowl stir together rice, cheese, the 2 to 3 tablespoons salsa, and cilantro.

Place a tortilla in a large nonstick skillet or griddle. Top with half of the rice mixture and half of the vegetables. Top with another tortilla. Cook over medium heat for 2 minutes or until cheese is nearly melted. Turn tortilla over carefully and cook 1 to 2 minutes more or until rice mixture is heated through. Remove quesadilla from skillet and repeat with remaining ingredients.

To serve, cut each quesadilla into 6 triangles. Serve with additional salsa.

Nutrition facts per serving: 360 cal., 15 g total fat (8 g sat. fat), 34 mg chol., 410 mg sodium, 41 g carbo., 3 g fiber, 16 g pro. Daily values: 48% vit. A, 41% vit. C, 28% calcium, 15% iron

Note: To cook rice, rinse and drain 1/2 cup wild rice. In a saucepan bring 1 1/2 cups water and 1/8 teaspoon salt to boiling. Add rice. Reduce heat and simmer, covered, 40 minutes or until rice is tender and most of the water is absorbed. Drain, if necessary. If desired, let cool, cover, and refrigerate for up to 3 days.

1½ **cups cooked wild rice***

1 **cup shredded asadero, queso quesadilla, or Monterey Jack cheese**

2 **to 3 tablespoons salsa**

1 **to 2 tablespoons snipped fresh cilantro**

4 **7- or 8-inch flour tortillas**

1 **cup chopped vegetables such as sweet pepper, carrots, zucchini, onion, and/or broccoli**

Salsa

spinach risotto
with acorn squash

Stubby Italian Arborio rice—the key to authentic risottos—creates a luscious dish. During cooking, the grains not only soften, but their special starch transforms the broth into a creamy, unforgettable sauce.

Start to finish: 30 minutes   Makes 4 servings

Cut each squash half crosswise into 1-inch slices. Cook, covered, in a small amount of boiling water for 10 to 15 minutes or until tender. Drain and keep warm.

Meanwhile, in a large saucepan cook onion and garlic in hot oil over medium heat about 4 minutes or until onion is tender. Add uncooked rice; cook and stir 1 minute more.

In a medium saucepan bring broth to boiling. Reduce heat and simmer. Slowly add 1 cup of the broth to the rice mixture, stirring constantly. Continue to cook and stir until liquid is absorbed. Add another ½ cup of the broth; continue to cook and stir until liquid is absorbed. Add another 1 cup broth, stirring constantly until broth has been absorbed. (This should take about 15 minutes.)

Stir in remaining ½ cup broth; cook and stir until rice is slightly creamy and just tender. Stir in spinach and Parmesan cheese. Serve risotto with squash slices.

Nutrition facts per serving: 296 cal., 6 g total fat (1 g sat. fat), 2 mg chol., 778 mg sodium, 60 g carbo., 5 g fiber, 8 g pro. Daily values: 129% vit. A, 59% vit. C, 12% calcium, 29% iron

1   1½-to 2-pound acorn or
    butternut squash, halved
    lengthwise and seeded

1   cup chopped red onion

4   cloves garlic, minced

1   tablespoon olive oil

1   cup Arborio rice or short-grain rice

3   cups vegetable or chicken broth

3   cups packed, chopped
    fresh spinach

2   tablespoons finely shredded
    Parmesan cheese

pasta
perfection

teriyaki penne

Served over pasta tubes, this easy Asian stir-fry delivers a tasty bonus with every bite. The zippy ginger-spiked sauce coats the pasta inside and out for a double dose of flavor.

Start to finish: 25 minutes   Makes 4 servings

Cook pasta according to package directions; drain.

Meanwhile, in a large skillet cook the ginger and garlic in hot oil for 15 seconds. Stir in shredded broccoli, mushrooms, and teriyaki sauce. Cook and stir about 5 minutes or until broccoli is crisp-tender.

To serve, toss broccoli mixture with hot pasta; add green onions.

Nutrition facts per serving: 286 cal., 5 g total fat (1 g sat. fat), 0 mg chol., 749 mg sodium, 50 g carbo., 5 g fiber, 11 g pro. Daily values: 14% vit. A, 72% vit. C, 3% calcium, 23% iron

- 8 ounces dried tomato-basil penne or plain mostaccioli pasta
- ½ teaspoon grated fresh ginger
- 1 clove garlic, minced
- 1 tablespoon toasted sesame oil or cooking oil
- 3 cups packaged shredded broccoli (broccoli slaw mix)
- 2 cups sliced fresh mushrooms
- ¼ cup teriyaki sauce
- ¼ cup thinly sliced green onions

caramelized onions
& garlic with cavatelli

In this piquant vegetable sauce for shell pasta, the ornery onion sheds its gruff nature, revealing an irresistible sweet other self. Tangy, syrupy Italian balsamic vinegar adds a subtle sophistication.

10 ounces dried cavatelli or other medium pasta (3½ cups)

2 medium onions, sliced (about 2 cups)

1 tablespoon olive oil

1 teaspoon sugar

1 medium zucchini, halved lengthwise and sliced

4 cloves garlic, minced

2 tablespoons water

1 to 2 tablespoons balsamic vinegar

¼ cup pine nuts or chopped walnuts, toasted

1 tablespoon snipped fresh thyme

Start to finish: 30 minutes   Makes 4 servings

Cook pasta according to package directions; drain and keep warm.

Meanwhile, in a large, heavy skillet cook onions, covered, in hot oil over medium-low heat for 13 to 15 minutes or until onions are tender. Uncover; add sugar. Cook and stir over medium-high heat for 4 to 5 minutes more or until onions are golden.

Add zucchini and garlic. Cook and stir for 2 minutes. Stir in water and vinegar; cook for 2 to 3 minutes more or until zucchini is crisp-tender.

To serve, in a large bowl toss together warm pasta, onion mixture, nuts, and thyme. If desired, season to taste with salt and pepper.

Nutrition facts per serving: 383 cal., 10 g total fat (1 g sat. fat), 0 mg chol., 5 mg sodium, 63 g carbo., 4 g fiber, 12 g pro. Daily values: 0% vit. A, 7% vit. C, 2% calcium, 26% iron

pasta ratatouille

No foreign travel or green thumb—just a quick trip to the grocery store—is required to savor this wonder of the Provençal kitchen garden. Add the aromatic punch of garlic-slathered baguette toasts and you'll swear you're dining in the south of France.

29

Start to finish: 25 minutes   Makes 4 servings

Cook pasta according to package directions; drain and keep warm.

Meanwhile, in a large saucepan heat oil over medium-high heat. Add eggplant; cook and stir for 1 minute. Add zucchini, yellow summer squash, onion, and sweet pepper; cook for 10 minutes more, stirring occasionally. Stir in pasta and undrained tomatoes. Serve immediately.

Nutrition facts per serving: 399 cal., 7 g total fat (1 g sat. fat), 0 mg chol., 501 mg sodium, 73 g carbo., 9 g fiber, 12 g pro. Daily values: 9% vit. A, 26% vit. C, 9% calcium, 26% iron

warming trend
Except in salads, pasta is best enjoyed hot from the pot. Always serve pasta in warmed, heat-conserving bowls. Use one of these easy methods to warm bowls: rinse them under hot water, splash them with pasta cooking water, or let them sit briefly in the oven at a low temperature.

- 10 ounces dried rigatoni or penne pasta
- 1 tablespoon olive oil
- 1 medium eggplant, peeled and cubed (5 cups)
- 1 medium zucchini, sliced (1¼ cups)
- 1 medium yellow summer squash, sliced (1¼ cups)
- 1 medium onion, chopped (½ cup)
- 1 medium green sweet pepper, chopped (½ cup)
- 1 15-ounce can chunky Italian-style tomatoes, undrained

cavatelli with arugula & dried cranberries

Unlike some other feasts that feature cranberries, this elegant pasta supper will leave you satisfied, but not stuffed. Peppery Italian arugula and pungent garlic punch up the sweetness of the dried fruit.

8 ounces dried cavatelli or rotini pasta (3 cups)

½ cup vegetable broth

2 cloves garlic, minced

1 tablespoon olive oil

4 cups torn arugula and/or fresh spinach

½ cup dried cranberries or raisins

½ cup sliced almonds or coarsely chopped pistachio nuts, toasted

¼ cup finely shredded Parmesan cheese

Start to finish: 20 minutes   Makes 4 servings

Cook pasta according to package directions; drain. Toss with broth and keep warm.

Meanwhile, in a large skillet cook garlic in hot oil over medium heat for 1 minute. Add arugula; cook and stir 1 to 2 minutes or until just wilted.

To serve, in a large bowl combine warm pasta mixture, arugula mixture, cranberries, and nuts. Toss gently to combine. Sprinkle each serving with Parmesan cheese. If desired, season to taste with salt or sea salt (as pictured opposite).

Nutrition facts per serving: 395 cal., 13 g total fat (1 g sat. fat), 5 mg chol., 331 mg sodium, 59 g carbo., 2 g fiber, 14 g pro. Daily values: 5% vit. A, 0% vit. C, 15% calcium, 21% iron

garlic asparagus & pasta with lemon cream

Delicate asparagus requires tender, loving care to show off its simple perfection. Providing just the coddling it needs are succulent baby squash, curly pasta ribbons, and a low-fuss, lemon-infused cream sauce.

Start to finish: 25 minutes   Makes 4 servings

Cook pasta according to package directions; drain and keep warm.

Meanwhile, melt margarine in a large skillet; add asparagus, squash, and garlic. Cook, stirring frequently, for 2 to 3 minutes or until vegetables are crisp-tender. Remove with a slotted spoon and add to pasta.

Combine whipping cream and lemon peel in skillet; bring to boiling. Boil for 2 to 3 minutes or until reduced to 1/3 cup. To serve, pour cream mixture over pasta mixture; toss gently to coat.

Nutrition facts per serving: 370 cal., 15 g total fat (8 g sat. fat), 41 mg chol., 49 mg sodium, 49 g carbo., 4 g fiber, 10 g pro. Daily values: 22% vit. A, 21% vit. C, 4% calcium, 18% iron

Note: One medium zucchini or yellow summer squash cut into 8 pieces may be substituted for the baby sunburst squash and/or pattypan squash.

- 8 ounces dried mafalda or rotini
- 1 tablespoon margarine or butter
- 2 cups asparagus cut into 2-inch pieces
- 8 baby sunburst squash and/or pattypan squash, halved (4 ounces)*
- 2 cloves garlic, minced
- ½ cup whipping cream
- 2 teaspoons finely shredded lemon peel

bow ties with olives & mint

Italians think of tiny wings, not neckwear, when they see the ruffled pasta they call farfalle (butterflies). Agreeable to any point of view is this simple Mediterranean mélange, refreshed with mint.

8 ounces dried bow tie pasta

¾ cup Greek black olives, pitted and halved, or pitted ripe olives, halved

2 plum tomatoes, seeded and chopped

¾ cup feta cheese or soft goat cheese (chèvre), crumbled

½ cup snipped fresh mint

1 tablespoon olive oil

¼ teaspoon pepper

Start to finish: 20 minutes   Makes 4 servings

Cook pasta according to package directions; drain.

Meanwhile, in a large bowl combine olives, tomatoes, cheese, and mint. Add pasta, olive oil, and pepper; toss gently to combine. Serve pasta mixture immediately or let it stand for up to 30 minutes.

Nutrition facts per serving: 322 cal., 14 g total fat (5 g sat. fat), 68 mg chol., 365 mg sodium, 40 g carbo., 3 g fiber, 11 g pro. Daily values: 8% vit. A, 20% vit. C, 12% calcium, 31% iron

a **plum tomato** by any **other name...**
Despite their resemblance to small pears, the best sauce tomatoes are called plum tomatoes or Romas. They are oval, meaty rather than juicy, and cook down to a thick, full-flavored sauce. To remove their few seeds, halve each crosswise, then give each half a gentle squeeze over a sink or bowl and the seeds will fall right out. Or, scoop out the seeds with a small spoon. Buy them canned when fresh are unavailable.

toasted garlic & orzo pilaf

Stand up to garlic's fearsome reputation. It mellows when cooked into a delectable seasoning, so add as much as you dare to this vibrant pilaf. Orzo is the pasta twin of rice, but with a more chewy texture.

Start to finish: 30 minutes   Makes 3 servings

In a medium saucepan cook garlic in hot oil over medium heat for 30 to 60 seconds or until light brown. Add orzo; cook and stir until orzo is light brown (do not let the garlic burn or it will become bitter).

Stir in rice. Slowly add broth and water. Bring to boiling. Reduce heat and simmer, covered, for 10 minutes. Stir in carrots, broccoli, and green onions. Simmer, covered, about 5 minutes more or until orzo and rice are tender and liquid is absorbed. To serve, if desired, season to taste with freshly ground pepper.

Nutrition facts per serving: 307 cal., 6 g total fat (1 g sat. fat), 0 mg chol., 605 mg sodium, 58 g carbo., 4 g fiber, 8 g pro. Daily values: 115% vit. A, 66% vit. C, 5% calcium, 23% iron

8 to 12 large cloves garlic, peeled and cut into thin slivers

1 tablespoon olive oil

½ cup orzo (rosamarina) pasta

½ cup long grain rice

1 14½-ounce can vegetable or chicken broth

¼ cup water

1 cup thinly sliced carrots

1 cup broccoli flowerets

¼ cup sliced green onions

couscous burritos

Moroccan pasta in a Mexican burrito? Why not! Let this speedy international wrap rocket your taste buds in an entirely new direction.

8 8-inch flavored or plain flour tortillas

1 cup vegetable or chicken broth

1 4-ounce can diced green chili
   peppers, drained

¼ teaspoon ground turmeric

  Dash pepper

⅔ cup quick-cooking couscous

¼ cup sliced green onions

1 cup chopped tomatoes

¾ cup chopped green sweet pepper

½ cup finely shredded reduced-fat
   Mexican-blend cheeses

  Salsa (optional)

Start to finish: 20 minutes   Makes 4 servings

Wrap the tortillas in foil. Heat in a 350° oven for 10 minutes to soften. (Or, wrap tortillas in microwave-safe paper towels. Microwave on high for 30 seconds.)

Meanwhile, in a small saucepan combine the broth, green chili peppers, turmeric, and pepper. Bring to boiling. Remove from heat and stir in couscous and green onions. Let stand, covered, for 5 minutes. Fluff couscous with a fork and stir in tomatoes and sweet pepper.

To assemble each burrito, spoon about ⅓ cup of the couscous mixture onto a tortilla just below center. Top with 2 tablespoons cheese. Roll up the tortilla. If desired, serve with salsa.

Nutrition facts per serving: 359 cal., 8 g total fat (3 g sat. fat), 5 mg chol., 661 mg sodium, 60 g carbo., 7 g fiber, 13 g pro. Daily values: 10% vit. A, 97% vit. C, 16% calcium, 19% iron

mostaccioli with
green beans & tomatoes

Most string beans are stringless these days, making this fresh vegetable sauce for pasta good and easy. A little white wine rounds out the sauce, and the flavor's just as full if you choose to substitute vegetable or chicken broth.

6 **ounces dried mostaccioli or penne pasta (about 2 cups)**

4 **ounces green beans and/or wax beans, cut into 1-inch pieces**

⅓ **cup chopped onion**

1 **clove garlic, minced**

2 **teaspoons olive oil**

3 **ripe medium plum tomatoes, seeded and chopped (about 1 cup)**

¼ **cup dry white wine, vegetable broth, or chicken broth**

2 **tablespoons finely shredded Parmesan cheese**

1 **tablespoon snipped fresh Italian parsley**

Start to finish: 30 minutes   Makes 3 servings

In a large saucepan cook pasta and beans in a large amount of lightly salted boiling water about 14 minutes or until the pasta and beans are tender. Drain; return to saucepan.

Meanwhile, in a medium saucepan cook onion and garlic in hot oil over medium heat for 2 to 3 minutes or until onion is tender. Reduce heat to low and add tomatoes and wine; cook and stir for 2 minutes more.

Add tomato mixture to pasta mixture; toss lightly to combine. Transfer to a serving dish. Sprinkle with Parmesan cheese and parsley. If desired, season to taste with freshly ground pepper.

Nutrition facts per serving: 313 cal. 6 g total fat (1 g sat. fat), 3 mg chol., 65 mg sodium, 52 g carbo., 3 g fiber, 11 g pro. Daily values: 8% vit. A, 33% vit. C, 6% calcium, 21% iron

penne with fennel

Because it tastes mildly of licorice, bulbous fennel is sometimes mislabeled "anise" in the supermarket. Fennel is at its sweetest in winter, making this casual supper the perfect cold-weather cure.

Start to finish: 30 minutes   Makes 4 servings

Cook pasta in a large saucepan according to package directions. Drain; return pasta to saucepan and keep warm.

Meanwhile, cut off and discard upper stalks of fennel bulbs. Remove any wilted outer layers of stalks. Wash fennel and cut lengthwise into quarters. Remove core; cut into thin strips.

In a large skillet cook the garlic and crushed red pepper in hot oil and margarine over medium-high heat for 30 seconds. Add fennel to skillet; cook and stir for 5 minutes. Add sweet pepper strips; cook 3 minutes more. Add beans and thyme; cook about 2 minutes or until hot.

To serve, add fennel mixture to pasta; toss gently to combine. If desired, season to taste with freshly ground pepper.

Nutrition facts per serving: 335 cal., 8 g total fat (1 g sat. fat), 0 mg chol., 128 mg sodium, 55 g carbo., 17 g fiber, 13 g pro. Daily values: 22% vit. A, 81% vit. C, 7% calcium, 23% iron

- 6 ounces dried penne pasta
- 2 medium fennel bulbs (about 2 pounds)
- 3 cloves garlic, minced
- ¼ teaspoon crushed red pepper
- 1 tablespoon olive oil or cooking oil
- 1 tablespoon margarine or butter
- 1 large red and/or green sweet pepper, cut into thin, bite-size strips (1 cup)
- 1 15-ounce can great Northern beans, rinsed and drained
- 1 teaspoon snipped fresh thyme

egg it on

egg ragout

This simple supper is the perfect conclusion to any weekend recreation, from a hike in the woods to a snooze on the couch. It's a scrumptious, creamy, egg-and-vegetable mélange that makes the most of pantry staples.

Start to finish: 25 minutes   Makes 4 servings

In a medium saucepan cook sugar snap peas and sunburst squash, covered, in a small amount of boiling salted water for 2 to 4 minutes or until crisp-tender; drain.

For sauce, in a large saucepan cook green onions in hot margarine until tender. Stir in flour. Add milk all at once. Cook and stir over medium heat until thickened and bubbly. Stir in Parmesan cheese and mustard; add cooked vegetables. Cook and stir about 1 minute more or until heated through. Gently stir in eggs. Serve over toasted bagels or bread.

Nutrition facts per serving: 392 cal., 13 g total fat (4 g sat. fat), 221 mg chol., 600 mg sodium, 49 g carbo., 1 g fiber, 19 g pro. Daily values: 22% vit. A, 33% vit. C, 19% calcium, 28% iron

Note: To cook the eggs, place them in a medium saucepan. Add enough cold water to come 1 inch above the eggs. Bring to boiling; reduce heat. Cover and simmer for 15 minutes; drain. Run cold water over eggs or place eggs in ice water until cool enough to handle; drain. Peel eggs. If desired, cover and refrigerate for up to 2 days.

1½ cups sugar snap peas, strings and tips removed

1 cup baby sunburst squash, cut into quarters

4 green onions, thinly bias-sliced

4 teaspoons margarine or butter

2 tablespoons all-purpose flour

1¼ cups milk

2 tablespoons grated Parmesan cheese

1 teaspoon sweet-hot mustard or Dijon-style mustard

4 hard-cooked eggs,* coarsely chopped

4 bagels, split and toasted or 4 slices whole wheat bread, toasted

broccoli omelet provençale

You don't need to own a classic omelet pan or be a French chef to whip up this bistro dish. Cooked in a rectangular baking pan, this omelet just might be the easiest version you'll ever make because the oven does all the work!

12   **eggs**

¼   **cup water**

½   **teaspoon garlic salt**

⅛   **teaspoon pepper**

    Nonstick spray coating

3   **cups packaged shredded broccoli (broccoli slaw mix)**

2   **tablespoons snipped fresh oregano or basil**

1   **10-ounce container refrigerated plum tomato pasta sauce, heated**

Start to finish: 20 minutes   Makes 6 servings

For omelet, in a large mixing bowl beat together eggs, water, garlic salt, and pepper. Spray a 15×10×1-inch baking pan with nonstick coating. Pour egg mixture into pan. Bake in a 400° oven about 7 minutes or until egg mixture is set, but still glossy and moist.

Meanwhile, place shredded broccoli in a steamer basket over boiling water; steam for 2 to 3 minutes or until heated through; stir in oregano.

To serve, cut omelet into six 5-inch squares. Transfer omelet squares to warm serving plates. Spoon some of the broccoli mixture on half of each omelet square; fold other half of omelet over filling. Spoon the warm pasta sauce over omelets. Serve immediately.

Nutrition facts per serving: 222 cal., 15 g total fat (6 g sat. fat), 439 mg chol., 454 mg sodium, 6 g carbo., 2 g fiber, 14 g pro. Daily values: 25% vit. A, 30% vit. C, 7% calcium, 11% iron

scrambled eggs fajitas

Dress is casual and dancing shoes are a must to stay in step with these festive roll-ups and their lively salsa beat. Set out the eggs and tortillas on a buffet table for easy self-service and blend up icy margaritas at the bar.

Start to finish: 25 minutes   Makes 6 servings

Wrap the tortillas in foil. Heat in a 350° oven for 10 minutes to soften. (Or, wrap tortillas in microwave-safe paper towels. Microwave on high for 30 seconds.)

Meanwhile, in a medium bowl beat together eggs, milk, salt, and pepper; set aside. In a large skillet cook and stir corn and jalapeño pepper in hot oil over medium heat for 2 to 4 minutes or until corn is tender.

Pour egg mixture over vegetables in skillet. Cook over medium heat, without stirring, until mixture begins to set on bottom and around edge. Using a spatula, lift and fold the partially cooked egg mixture so the uncooked portion flows underneath. Add cheese. Continue cooking over medium heat until egg mixture is cooked through, but still glossy and moist. Remove from heat. Sprinkle with green onion and cilantro.

To serve, fill warmed tortillas with egg mixture; roll up. Serve with salsa.

Nutrition facts per serving: 263 cal., 11 g total fat (3 g sat. fat), 221 mg chol., 398 mg sodium, 27 g carbo., 0 g fiber, 13 g pro. Daily values: 15% vit. A, 17% vit. C, 13% calcium, 14% iron

6 7-inch flour tortillas

6 eggs

⅓ cup milk

⅛ teaspoon salt

⅛ teaspoon pepper

1 cup frozen whole kernel corn

1 jalapeño pepper, seeded
and finely chopped

2 teaspoons cooking oil

½ cup shredded reduced-fat
Monterey Jack or
cheddar cheese

2 tablespoons thinly sliced
green onion

2 tablespoons snipped fresh cilantro

Salsa

southwest skillet

It's home on the range with a stove-top main course built on classic southwestern flavors. Round up everything you need in the aisles of most supermarkets.

2 tablespoons sliced almonds

1 yellow sweet pepper, cut into
    thin, bite-size strips

1 jalapeño pepper, seeded
    and chopped

1 tablespoon olive oil or cooking oil

4 medium tomatoes (about
    1¼ pounds), peeled and chopped

1½ to 2 teaspoons purchased or
    homemade Mexican Seasoning*

¼ teaspoon salt

4 eggs

1 medium ripe avocado, seeded,
    peeled, and sliced (optional)

Fresh chili peppers (optional)

Start to finish: 25 minutes   Makes 4 servings

Spread almonds in a large skillet. Cook, stirring occasionally, over medium heat for 4 to 5 minutes or until lightly browned. Remove toasted almonds from skillet; set aside. In the same skillet cook sweet pepper and jalapeño pepper in hot oil about 2 minutes or until tender. Stir in tomatoes, Mexican seasoning, and salt. Bring to boiling. Reduce heat and simmer, covered, for 5 minutes.

Break one of the eggs into a measuring cup. Carefully slide the egg into simmering tomato mixture. Repeat with remaining eggs. Sprinkle the eggs lightly with salt and pepper.

Cover and simmer eggs over medium-low heat for 3 to 5 minutes or until the whites are completely set and yolks begin to thicken but are not firm. To serve, transfer eggs to serving plates with a slotted spoon. Stir mixture in skillet; spoon around eggs on plates. Sprinkle with the toasted almonds. If desired, serve with avocado slices and garnish with fresh chili peppers.

Nutrition facts per serving: 166 cal., 11 g total fat (2 g sat. fat), 213 mg chol., 216 mg sodium, 10 g carbo., 2 g fiber, 9 g pro. Daily values: 20% vit. A, 126% vit. C, 4% calcium, 12% iron

Note: For homemade Mexican seasoning, combine 1 to 1½ teaspoons chili powder and ½ teaspoon ground cumin.

autumn frittata

Along with acorns and blazing leaves, the centerpiece of an autumn brunch should be this delicious dish infused with the seasonal flavors of fennel and sweet potatoes.

6 eggs

1 tablespoon snipped fresh
   chervil or parsley

¼ teaspoon salt

1 medium fennel bulb, thinly
   sliced (about 1 cup)

1 large sweet onion (such as Vidalia
   or Walla Walla), thinly sliced

2 tablespoons olive oil

3 medium sweet potatoes (1 pound),
   cooked, peeled, and thinly
   sliced,* or one 16-ounce can
   sweet potatoes, drained
   and sliced

Prep: 15 minutes   Bake: 18 minutes   Makes 4 servings

In a medium bowl beat eggs, chervil, and salt; set aside.

In a 10-inch ovenproof skillet cook and stir fennel and onion in hot oil for 5 to 7 minutes or until vegetables are tender. Layer sliced sweet potatoes on top of fennel and onion in skillet. Pour egg mixture into skillet.

Bake in a 350° oven for 18 to 20 minutes or until a knife inserted near the center comes out clean. Serve immediately.

Nutrition facts per serving: 283 cal., 14 g total fat (3 g sat. fat), 320 mg chol., 249 mg sodium, 27 g carbo., 9 g fiber, 12 g pro. Daily values: 207% vit. A, 45% vit. C, 6% calcium, 10% iron

Note: Cook sweet potatoes, covered, in enough boiling water to cover, for 25 to 35 minutes or until tender. Drain; cool slightly before peeling and slicing.

cookware that **handles** the **heat**
Most skillets meant for stove-top use are also ovenproof, but are their handles? Make sure that your skillet handle can withstand the high heat before using it in the oven. If in doubt, wrap its handle in a couple of layers of heavy-duty foil or select a skillet with a removable handle.

potatoes & eggs

If you enjoy a side of potatoes with your eggs, this omelet goes one better. It mixes them together so you get both with every forkful, plus garden-fresh bits of crunchy asparagus and juicy tomato.

Start to finish: 30 minutes   Makes 6 servings

In a large nonstick skillet cook potatoes, covered, in a small amount of boiling water for 5 minutes. Add asparagus; cover and cook for 5 to 7 minutes more or until vegetables are tender; drain. Cool skillet slightly; wipe with paper towels. Spray skillet with nonstick coating. Return vegetables to skillet.

In a medium mixing bowl combine eggs, Parmesan cheese, rosemary, onion powder, salt, and pepper; pour over vegetables in skillet. Cook over medium heat, without stirring, until the egg mixture begins to set on bottom and around edge. Using a spatula, lift and fold the partially cooked egg mixture so uncooked portion flows underneath. Continue cooking over medium heat until the egg mixture is set, but still glossy and moist.

Remove egg mixture skillet from heat. Cover and let stand for 3 to 4 minutes or until top is set. To serve, divide mixture among 6 plates; top each serving with chopped tomato.

Nutrition facts per serving: 128 cal., 6 g total fat (2 g sat. fat), 213 mg chol., 171 mg sodium, 11 g carbo., 1 g fiber, 8 g pro. Daily values: 13% vit. A, 26% vit. C, 4% calcium, 11% iron

8 ounces whole tiny new potatoes, cut into ¼-inch-thick slices

1 cup asparagus, cut into ½-inch pieces

Nonstick spray coating

6 beaten eggs

1 tablespoon finely shredded or grated Parmesan cheese

1 teaspoon snipped fresh rosemary

¼ teaspoon onion powder

¼ teaspoon salt

¼ teaspoon pepper

1 large tomato, seeded and coarsely chopped

corn & tomato
bread pudding

The proof of a delicious dinner is in this pudding, a classic baked custard dessert reinvented as a savory main course. Cut cubes from only firm, day-old (or older) bread, as fresh bread is too soft to soak up all the milk and eggs and hold its shape.

49

Prep: 20 minutes   Bake: 30 minutes   Makes 6 servings

Place dried tomatoes in a small bowl; add enough hot water to cover. Let stand about 15 minutes or until softened; drain.

Meanwhile, in a medium bowl beat together eggs, milk, and basil; set aside. In an ungreased 2-quart square baking dish toss together torn English muffins, corn, cheese, and softened tomatoes.* Carefully pour egg mixture evenly over mixture in baking dish.

Bake in a 375° oven about 30 minutes or until a knife inserted near the center comes out clean. Cool slightly. To serve, if desired, spoon bread pudding atop tomato wedges.

Nutrition facts per serving: 275 cal., 9 g total fat (4 g sat. fat), 160 mg chol., 486 mg sodium, 32 g carbo., 3 g fiber, 16 g pro. Daily values: 14% vit. A, 6% vit. C, 23% calcium, 11% iron

To make-ahead: Cover and refrigerate the egg mixture and English muffin mixture separately for up to 24 hours. Combine and bake as directed.

3 tablespoons snipped dried tomatoes (not oil-packed)

4 beaten eggs

1½ cups milk, half-and-half, or light cream

1 tablespoon snipped fresh basil or 1 teaspoon dried basil, crushed

4 cups torn English muffins or dry French bread

1½ cups fresh or frozen whole kernel corn

1 cup shredded reduced-fat cheddar cheese or hot pepper cheese (4 ounces)

1 tomato, cut into thin wedges (optional)

garlic couscous
with **eggs** & salsa

Using preseasoned couscous instead of plain adds flavor and subtracts steps, appeasing both appetites and the clock on a busy day. Balsamic vinegar elevates a simple vegetable salsa notches above the usual.

1 **5.8-ounce package roasted garlic and olive oil couscous, toasted pine nut couscous, or tomato-lentil couscous, or ⅔ cup plain couscous**

1 **cup chopped tomato**

1 **cup chopped zucchini**

2 **teaspoons olive oil**

1 **teaspoon balsamic vinegar**

1 **clove garlic, minced**

1 **tablespoon margarine or butter**

4 **eggs, beaten**

Start to finish: 25 minutes   Makes 4 servings

Prepare couscous according to package directions.

Meanwhile, for salsa, in a small mixing bowl stir together tomato, zucchini, oil, vinegar, and garlic; set aside.

In a medium skillet melt margarine over medium heat; pour in eggs. Cook eggs over medium heat, without stirring, until eggs begin to set on the bottom and around edge.

Using a spatula, lift and fold the partially cooked eggs so the uncooked portion flows underneath. Continue cooking over medium heat for 2 to 3 minutes or until eggs are cooked through, but still glossy and moist. Remove from heat. Stir eggs into couscous. Season to taste with salt and pepper. Serve with salsa.

Nutrition facts per serving: 289 cal., 11 g total fat (2 g sat. fat), 213 mg chol., 496 mg sodium, 35 g carbo., 2 g fiber, 12 g pro. Daily values: 17% vit. A, 23% vit. C, 2% calcium, 11% iron

bravo **balsamico!**
Balsamic vinegar develops its intense, sweet-tart flavor through years of pampered rest in casks of differing woods. The most prized elixirs are concocted in the Italian city of Modena following ancient secret formulas. More a condiment than a cooking liquid, balsamic vinegar should be savored in small amounts.

tomato & asparagus pizza

Eggs scrambled with fresh herbs and garden vegetables aren't just for breakfast. They make a great topping for an anytime pizza, too. A prepared crust trims preparation time.

Start to finish: 20 minutes   Makes 6 servings

Place bread shell on a 12-inch pizza pan. Bake in a 450° oven for 8 to 10 minutes or until heated through.

Meanwhile, in a mixing bowl beat together eggs, milk, tarragon, salt, and pepper. In a large skillet cook asparagus and garlic in hot margarine over medium heat for 3 minutes; pour egg mixture over asparagus mixture in skillet. Cook over medium heat, without stirring, until mixture begins to set on the bottom and around edge.

Using a spatula, lift and fold the partially cooked egg mixture so the uncooked portion flows underneath. Continue cooking over medium heat for 2 to 3 minutes or until egg mixture is cooked through, but still glossy and moist. Remove from heat.

Arrange tomato slices evenly around the edge of the baked bread shell. Spoon scrambled egg mixture in the center. Serve immediately.

Nutrition facts per serving: 327 cal., 14 g total fat (2 g sat. fat), 217 mg chol., 575 mg sodium, 36 g carbo., 2 g fiber, 16 g pro. Daily values: 18% vit. A, 17% vit. C, 10% calcium, 16% iron

1 12-inch Italian bread shell (Boboli)

6 eggs

⅓ cup milk

2 teaspoons snipped fresh tarragon
     or oregano

⅛ teaspoon salt

⅛ teaspoon pepper

1 cup asparagus bias-sliced into
     1-inch pieces

1 clove garlic, minced

2 tablespoons margarine or butter

1 large tomato, halved and sliced

moo shu vegetable
& egg crepes

If there's ever a Chinese take-out Hall of Fame, this menu all-star would surely be in it. A speedy home-cooked rendition, expedited by a sweet-and-sour sauce that starts in a bottle and finishes in a second, delivers dinner in short order.

12 asparagus spears, cut into
    3-inch pieces

2 medium carrots, cut into thin,
    3-inch-long julienne strips

2 green onions, cut into 2-inch pieces

3 tablespoons sweet-and-sour sauce

1 tablespoon orange juice or
    pineapple juice

1 teaspoon grated fresh ginger

5 eggs

¼ cup water

1 tablespoon cooking oil

Start to finish: 30 minutes   Makes 3 servings

In a large saucepan cook the asparagus, carrots, and green onions in a small amount of boiling lightly salted water for 7 to 9 minutes or until vegetables are crisp-tender; drain.

Meanwhile, for sauce, in a small mixing bowl stir together sweet-and-sour sauce, orange juice, and ginger; set aside.

For egg crepes, beat eggs and water until combined but not frothy. In an 8- or 10-inch nonstick skillet with flared sides, heat 1 teaspoon of the oil until a drop of water sizzles. Lift and tilt skillet to coat sides with oil. Add about ½ cup of the egg mixture to skillet. Cook over medium heat, without stirring, until mixture begins to set on bottom and around edge. Using a spatula, lift and fold the partially cooked egg mixture so the uncooked portion flows underneath. When mixture is set, but still shiny and moist, remove skillet from heat. Repeat to make two more crepes.

Spread about 2 teaspoons sauce onto center of each crepe. Arrange one-third of the vegetables on one-quarter of the crepe. Fold crepe in half over the vegetables; fold in half again. Serve with remaining sauce.

Nutrition facts per serving: 223 cal., 13 g total fat (3 g sat. fat), 355 mg chol., 188 mg sodium, 13 g carbo., 2 g fiber, 12 g pro. Daily values: 134% vit. A, 26% vit. C, 5% calcium, 11% iron

egg salad with lemon aioli

Indulge your artistic inclinations and also your appetite with a substantial egg salad that composes like a still life and tastes like Provence. No such dish is complete without aioli (ay-OH-lee), the classic Provençal garlic mayonnaise.

¼ cup light mayonnaise dressing

2 to 3 tablespoons milk

½ teaspoon finely shredded lemon peel

2 teaspoons lemon juice

1 to 2 cloves garlic, minced

2 cups shredded radicchio

4 to 6 hard-cooked eggs,* quartered

1 medium carrot, thinly bias-sliced

1 medium ripe avocado, seeded, peeled, and chopped (optional)

2 tablespoons chopped peanuts or cashews

4 ¾-inch-thick slices French bread, toasted

Start to finish: 30 minutes   Makes 4 servings

For aioli, in a medium bowl stir together mayonnaise and milk. Stir in lemon peel, lemon juice, and garlic; set aside.

Divide radicchio among 4 salad plates. Top radicchio with eggs, carrots, and, if desired, avocado. Sprinkle with peanuts. Spoon aioli over salads. Serve with toasted bread.

Nutrition facts per serving: 241 cal., 14 g total fat (3 g sat. fat), 214 mg chol., 375 mg sodium, 19 g carbo., 1 g fiber, 10 g pro. Daily values: 59% vit. A, 8% vit. C, 5% calcium, 9% iron

Note: To cook the eggs, place them in a medium saucepan. Add enough cold water to come 1 inch above the eggs. Bring to boiling; reduce heat. Cover and simmer for 15 minutes; drain. Run cold water over the eggs or place eggs in ice water until cool enough to handle; drain. Peel eggs. If desired, cover and refrigerate for up to 2 days.

egg & apple bruschetta

Never so humble is always special garlic toast Italian style—better known as bruschetta (broo-SKEH-tah). Start with a country loaf of bread that has a crispy crust. Then pile on eggs, apples, and nuts tossed with tangy blue cheese dressing.

55

Prep: 25 minutes   Makes 4 servings

Stir together oil and garlic. Using a pastry brush, brush some of the oil mixture over one side of each bread slice. Place bread slices on a baking sheet. Bake in a 450° oven about 10 minutes or until tops of bread slices are golden brown.

Meanwhile, in a medium mixing bowl toss together the eggs, apple, walnuts, and salad dressing. Top each toasted bread slice with some of the egg mixture. Serve immediately.

Nutrition facts per serving: 213 cal., 12 g total fat (2 g sat. fat), 162 mg chol., 288 mg sodium, 19 g carbo., 1 g fiber, 8 g pro. Daily values: 6% vit. A, 2% vit. C, 4% calcium, 8% iron

2 teaspoons olive oil

1 clove garlic, minced

4 1-inch-thick slices crusty white bread or twelve ½-inch-thick slices baguette-style French bread

3 hard-cooked eggs, chopped (see note, page 54)

¾ cup shredded tart apple

2 tablespoons toasted chopped walnuts

2 tablespoons bottled blue cheese salad dressing

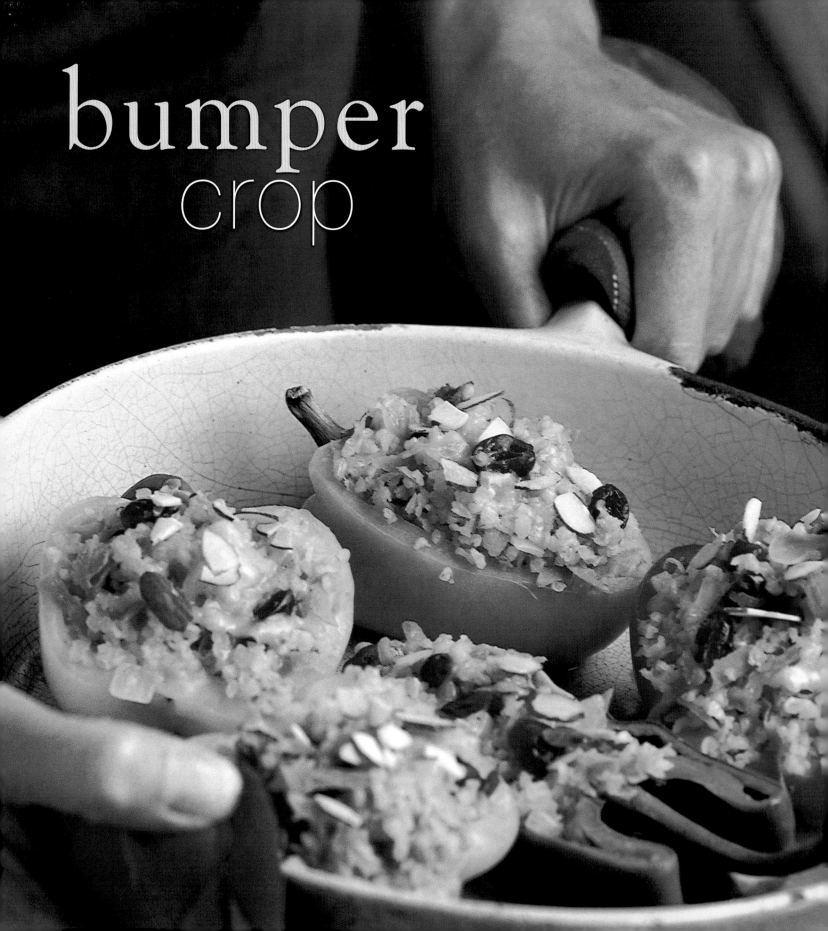

bumper
crop

peppers stuffed
with cinnamon bulgur

This easy stove-top supper—full of Middle Eastern flavors—can appear on your table in half the time of most stuffed-pepper entrées, so it's a good choice on even the busiest of days.

Start to finish: 30 minutes   Makes 4 servings

In a large skillet stir together the 1¾ cups water, carrot, onion, bouillon granules, salt, and cinnamon. Bring to boiling. Reduce heat and simmer, covered, for 5 minutes. Stir in bulgur and cranberries. Remove from heat. Cover and let stand for 5 minutes. If using stick cinnamon, remove from the bulgur mixture. Drain off excess liquid.

Meanwhile, halve the sweet peppers lengthwise, removing the seeds and membranes.

Stir shredded cheese into bulgur mixture; spoon into sweet pepper halves. Place sweet pepper halves in skillet. Add the ½ cup water. Bring to boiling. Reduce heat and simmer, covered, for 5 to 10 minutes or until sweet peppers are crisp-tender and bulgur mixture is heated through. Sprinkle with nuts.

Nutrition facts per serving: 250 cal., 9 g total fat (4 g sat. fat), 20 mg chol., 432 mg sodium, 35 g carbo., 8 g fiber, 10 g pro. Daily values: 82% vit. A, 141% vit. C, 15% calcium, 9% iron

Note: Four large poblano peppers may be substituted for the the sweet peppers. Prepare as directed above.

1¾ cups water

½ cup shredded carrot

¼ cup chopped onion

1 teaspoon instant vegetable or chicken bouillon granules

⅛ teaspoon salt

3 inches stick cinnamon or dash ground cinnamon

¾ cup bulgur

⅓ cup dried cranberries or raisins

2 large or 4 small sweet peppers, any color*

¾ cup shredded Muenster, brick, or mozzarella cheese

½ cup water

2 tablespoons sliced almonds or chopped pecans, toasted

roasted asparagus with new potatoes

If you've never made asparagus this way before, you'll wonder why you waited! Its natural flavor not only survives the high oven heat, but thrives on it, emerging deeper, richer, and better than ever.

58

1 pound asparagus spears

1¼ pounds whole tiny new potatoes, cut into ½-inch pieces

1 tablespoon olive oil

¼ teaspoon salt

1 teaspoon snipped fresh rosemary

¼ teaspoon pepper

⅓ cup shredded Parmesan cheese

¼ cup pine nuts, toasted

Start to finish: 35 minutes   Makes 4 servings

Snap off and discard woody bases from asparagus.

In a roasting pan toss asparagus and potatoes with oil; sprinkle with salt. Spread asparagus and potatoes in a single layer in the roasting pan.

Roast in a 450° oven for 10 to 15 minutes or until asparagus and potatoes are just tender. Stir in rosemary and pepper. To serve, sprinkle with Parmesan cheese and pine nuts. Serve warm.

Nutrition facts per serving: 275 cal., 11 g total fat (1 g sat. fat), 7 mg chol., 266 mg sodium, 36 g carbo., 3 g fiber, 12 g pro. Daily values: 6% vit. A, 60% vit. C, 10% calcium, 24% iron

how to **pick** an **olive oil**
Extra-virgin olive oils are cold-pressed for highest quality and full-bodied flavor, but they aren't always the best choice for cooking. For stir-fries and sautés, use a virgin olive oil or pure olive oil as they're less affected by heat (and more economical). Reserve costly premium olive oils for salad dressings and fresh sauces where their fruity flavor can shine through.

vegetable & tofu stir-fry

Made from soybeans, highly nutritious tofu—or bean curd—comes in a number of market forms. Soft tofu (Japanese style) works best in delicate soups and simmered dishes. Choose firm tofu (Chinese style) for tasty stir-fries such as this one.

Start to finish: 30 minutes   Makes 4 servings

Prepare rice according to package directions; keep warm.

For sauce, in a small mixing bowl stir together the broth, dry sherry, cornstarch, soy sauce, sugar, ginger, and, if desired, crushed red pepper. Set sauce aside.

Spray a cold wok or large skillet with nonstick coating. Preheat over medium-high heat. Stir-fry carrots and garlic for 2 minutes. Add broccoli; stir-fry 3 to 4 minutes more or until vegetables are crisp-tender. Push vegetables from center of wok.

Stir sauce; add to center of wok. Cook and stir until thickened and bubbly. Add tofu; stir together tofu and vegetables to coat with sauce. Cook and stir for 1 minute more.

To serve, spoon vegetable mixture over rice.

Nutrition facts per serving: 187 cal., 3 g total fat (0 g sat. fat), 0 mg chol., 306 mg sodium, 33 g carbo., 5 g fiber, 8 g pro. Daily values: 89% vit. A, 84% vit. C, 4% calcium, 10% iron

1½ **cups quick-cooking brown rice**

½ **cup vegetable or chicken broth**

¼ **cup dry sherry**

1 **tablespoon cornstarch**

1 **tablespoon reduced-sodium soy sauce**

1 **teaspoon sugar**

1 **teaspoon grated fresh ginger**

½ **teaspoon crushed red pepper (optional)**

Nonstick spray coating

1 **cup thinly sliced carrots**

3 **cloves garlic, minced**

3 **cups broccoli flowerets**

6 **ounces tofu (fresh bean curd), cut in ½-inch cubes**

indian-spiced squash

Everyone's the cook when it comes to a curry, and this vegetarian version proves why. Its array of traditional condiments lets diners season to taste at the table, so no two mouthfuls are ever the same.

¼ cup shelled raw pumpkin
   seeds (pepitas)

1 tablespoon grated fresh ginger

2 tablespoons olive oil

2 pounds winter squash, peeled,
   seeded, and cut into ½-inch
   pieces (about 4 cups)

½ cup dried cranberries or raisins

1 teaspoon ground cinnamon

1 teaspoon ground coriander

½ teaspoon ground cumin

½ teaspoon curry powder

1 14½-ounce can vegetable
   or chicken broth

4 cups hot cooked brown rice

   Condiments such as sliced
   bananas, pineapple chunks,
   sliced green onions, and/or
   chutney (optional)

Start to finish: 30 minutes   Makes 4 servings

In a large skillet toast pumpkin seeds over medium heat 4 to 5 minutes or until puffed and lightly browned, stirring occasionally. (Watch carefully as pumpkin seeds may pop in skillet.) Remove from skillet; set aside.

In the same skillet cook and stir ginger in hot oil over medium heat for 1 minute. Increase heat to medium-high; add squash and cook for 3 to 5 minutes or until squash starts to brown. Add the cranberries, cinnamon, coriander, cumin, and curry powder; cook for 1 minute more.

Carefully add broth to squash mixture. Bring to boiling. Reduce heat and cook, covered, for 10 to 15 minutes or until squash is tender, but not mushy. To serve, spoon over rice and sprinkle with pumpkin seeds. If desired, pass condiments.

Nutrition facts per serving: 450 cal., 13 g total fat (2 g sat. fat), 0 mg chol., 441 mg sodium, 81 g carbo., 9 g fiber, 9 g pro. Daily values: 134% vit. A, 48% vit. C, 9% calcium, 27% iron

roasted vegetables parmesan

These simply seasoned vegetables are hot! They're a delectable toss of zucchini, onion, sweet pepper, mushrooms, and carrots; tomatoes and garbanzo beans are stirred in during the final minutes in the oven. Grate your own Parmesan for the most flavor.

2 medium zucchini, cut into 1-inch chunks

1 medium onion, cut into 8 wedges

1 medium red or green sweet pepper, cut into 1-inch chunks

8 ounces mushrooms, stems removed

1 cup baby carrots

1 tablespoon olive oil

½ teaspoon salt

1 15-ounce can garbanzo beans, rinsed and drained

1 14½-ounce can diced tomatoes with garlic and Italian herbs

½ cup shredded Parmesan cheese

Prep: 15 minutes   Roast: 22 minutes   Makes 6 servings

In a large roasting pan combine zucchini, onion, sweet pepper, mushrooms, and carrots. Drizzle with oil. Toss to coat. Spread evenly in the roasting pan. Sprinkle with salt.

Roast vegetables in a 500° oven 12 minutes. Remove from oven; stir in beans and tomatoes. Reduce heat to 375°. Roast, uncovered, 10 minutes more or until heated through. To serve, sprinkle with cheese.

Nutrition facts per serving: 160 cal., 6 g total fat (0 g sat. fat), 7 mg chol., 867 mg sodium, 20 g carbo., 5 g fiber, 8 g pro. Daily values: 69% vit. A, 63% vit. C, 11% calcium, 16% iron

grilled vegetables
with onion sauce

A savory onion-flavored sauce carries the vegetable theme of this simple dish to its logical—and tasty—conclusion. Pour it in a sauce boat and pass alongside the piled-high platter of grilled veggies. Add steaming rice or couscous if you like.

Prep: 25 minutes   Makes 4 servings

In a medium saucepan cook potato wedges, covered, in boiling water for 4 minutes; drain. Drizzle potatoes, zucchini, and sweet peppers with oil. Grill vegetables on the greased rack of an uncovered grill directly over medium coals about 10 minutes or until tender.

Meanwhile, in a small saucepan cook onion and garlic in hot margarine over medium heat about 4 minutes or until onions are tender. Stir in cornstarch, sugar, and salt. Gradually stir in beer and broth. Cook and stir over medium heat until thickened and bubbly. Cook and stir for 2 minutes more. Remove from heat. Serve with vegetables.

Nutrition facts per serving: 244 cal., 7 g total fat (1 g sat. fat), 0 mg chol., 299 mg sodium, 42 g carbo., 3 g fiber, 4 g pro. Daily values: 47% vit. A, 194% vit. C, 3% calcium, 14% iron

- 3 **medium baking potatoes (about 1 pound), cut lengthwise into 8 wedges**
- 4 **small zucchini, halved lengthwise**
- 3 **medium red or green sweet peppers, cut into 4 wedges**
- 1 **tablespoon olive oil**
- 1 **cup chopped onion**
- 1 **clove garlic, minced**
- 1 **tablespoon margarine or butter**
- 1 **tablespoon cornstarch**
- ½ **teaspoon sugar**
- ¼ **teaspoon salt**
- ⅔ **cup dark beer, or dark or amber nonalcoholic beer**
- ½ **cup vegetable or chicken broth**

warm **beet** salad with roasted garlic dressing

Garlic groupies—this stellar salad has your name on it, spelled out in a garlic-spiked dressing for succulent beets and crunchy green beans. Serve the vegetables warm so they absorb the sauce to the fullest.

Start to finish: 30 minutes   Makes 4 servings

In a large saucepan cook green beans, covered, in a small amount of lightly salted boiling water about 15 minutes or until almost tender. Add beets and cook for 2 to 3 minutes more or until beets are heated through. Drain and keep warm.

Meanwhile, for dressing,* in a screw-top jar combine orange juice, oil, vinegar, garlic, and salt. Cover and shake well. Pour dressing over warm beans and beets. Spread cream cheese over French bread slices.

To serve, divide salad greens among 4 plates. Top with warm or room temperature beet mixture accompanied by French bread. If desired, sprinkle salads with coarsely ground pepper.

Nutrition facts per serving: 320 cal., 13 g total fat (4 g sat. fat), 12 mg chol., 632 mg sodium, 43 g carbo., 4 g fiber, 8 g pro. Daily values: 10% vit. A, 32% vit. C, 10% calcium, 27% iron

Note: In place of the homemade dressing, you can substitute a bottled garlic salad dressing or stir the bottled roasted minced garlic into a bottled Italian salad dressing.

1 **pound fresh green beans**

1 **16-ounce can sliced beets, drained**

2 **tablespoons orange juice**

2 **tablespoons olive oil**

1 **tablespoon balsamic vinegar**

2 **teaspoons bottled roasted minced garlic**

⅛ **teaspoon salt**

¼ **cup soft-style herbed cream cheese or ¼ cup spreadable Brie cheese**

8 **slices French bread, lightly toasted**

Purchased mixed salad greens

wheat berry tabouleh

To make a more substantial salad, this version of a Middle Eastern classic uses beanlike wheat berries instead of the usual cracked wheat, which is lighter and fluffier. Look for wheat berries where natural foods are sold.

2⅔ cups cooked wheat berries

¾ cup chopped tomato

¾ cup chopped cucumber

½ cup snipped fresh parsley

¼ cup thinly sliced green onions

1 tablespoon snipped fresh mint

3 tablespoons cooking oil

3 tablespoons lemon juice

¼ teaspoon salt

4 lettuce leaves

Pita chips (optional)

Prep: 25 minutes   Makes 4 servings

In a large bowl combine cooked wheat berries, tomato, cucumber, parsley, green onions, and mint.

For dressing, in a screw-top jar combine oil, lemon juice, and salt. Cover and shake well. Drizzle dressing over wheat berry mixture; toss to coat. Serve immediately or cover and chill for up to 24 hours.

Serve on lettuce-lined plates with pita chips, if desired.

Nutrition facts per serving: 269 cal., 12 g total fat (2 g sat. fat), 0 mg chol., 565 mg sodium, 39 g carbo., 3 g fiber, 8 g pro. Daily values: 9% vit. A, 44% vit. C, 2% calcium, 19% iron

Note: To cook wheat berries, bring one 14½-ounce can vegetable or chicken broth and ¼ cup water to boiling. Add 1 cup wheat berries; return to boiling. Reduce heat and simmer, covered, about 1 hour or until tender; drain. Cover and refrigerate up to 3 days.

wilted greens with dried tomatoes & pasta

Five o'clock and clueless as to what to have for dinner? Let pasta tossed with dried tomatoes, vitamin-rich greens, and a hefty dose of garlic solve the dilemma. Consider elephant garlic for this recipe—the cloves are larger and easier to slice.

Start to finish: 25 minutes   Makes 4 servings

In a large saucepan cook pasta according to package directions, adding garlic the last 4 minutes of cooking; drain. Return pasta and garlic to pan.

Meanwhile, drain tomatoes, reserving 1 tablespoon oil. Cut tomatoes into strips. Add tomato strips, reserved oil, spinach, salt, and pepper to pasta in pan; toss gently to combine. Cover pan for 2 minutes* or until spinach is slightly wilted. Sprinkle with feta cheese. Serve warm.

Nutrition facts per serving: 248 cal., 6 g total fat (3 g sat. fat), 14 mg chol., 336 mg sodium, 40 g carbo., 3 g fiber, 11 g pro. Daily values: 59% vit. A, 56% vit. C, 14% calcium, 27% iron

Note: If using beet greens or Swiss chard, cover pan and cook over medium heat for 2 to 3 minutes or until greens are slightly wilted and tender.

- 6 **ounces dried orecchiette pasta (about 1¾ cups) or dried small shell macaroni (about 1⅔ cups)**
- 4 **cloves garlic, thinly sliced**
- ⅓ **cup oil-packed dried tomatoes**
- 6 **cups torn fresh spinach, beet greens, or Swiss chard**
- ⅛ **teaspoon salt**
- ⅛ **teaspoon coarsely ground pepper**
- ¼ **cup crumbled feta cheese**

dried tomato tactics

You'll find dark-red, flavor-rich nuggets of dried tomatoes as halves or bits, dry or marinated in oil. Marinated dried tomatoes are ready to use once drained, but plain ones need plumping: Cover them with boiling water, let stand 5 minutes, then drain and pat dry. Snip into pieces with scissors if needed.

papaya & olives
with brown rice

As payback for the extra minutes it takes to cook, brown rice rewards with the full dietary benefits of the whole grain—including the nutritious bran that white rice sheds when polished.

3 cups cooked brown rice*

¼ cup chopped papaya or mango

3 tablespoons pitted ripe olives, coarsely chopped

2 tablespoons snipped fresh chives

2 tablespoons balsamic vinegar

1 tablespoon olive oil

3 tablespoons slivered almonds, toasted

Lettuce leaves

1 to 2 papayas, seeded and cut into wedges

Start to finish: 15 minutes   Makes 3 servings

In a large bowl combine cooked rice, papaya, olives, chives, vinegar, and oil; toss to combine.

Serve immediately or cover and chill for up to 6 hours.

Just before serving, stir in almonds. Serve on lettuce-lined plates with papaya wedges.

Nutrition facts per serving: 357 cal., 12 g total fat (2 g sat. fat), 0 mg chol., 55 mg sodium, 57 g carbo., 5 g fiber, 8 g pro. Daily values: 13% vit. A, 68% vit. C, 5% calcium, 13% iron

Note: To cook brown rice, in a medium saucepan bring 2 cups water and ¼ teaspoon salt to boiling. Add 1 cup rice. Return to boiling. Reduce heat and simmer, covered, for 45 minutes. Let stand for 5 minutes. If desired, cover and chill for up to 3 days.

great greens with cashews

It's easy to be green these days. This lively salad sampler mixes new and familiar textures and tastes from the produce aisle. Adding crunch are roasted cashews that fortify the dressing and also add flavor.

¾ **cup lightly salted roasted cashews**

½ **cup water**

 1 **small clove garlic, halved**

¼ **teaspoon salt**

⅛ **teaspoon onion powder**

 2 **tablespoons lemon juice**

 5 **cups torn mixed salad greens, such as romaine, arugula, leaf lettuce, radicchio, and/or curly endive**

1½ **cups chopped tomato**

 1 **cup frozen peas**

⅓ **cup raisins**

 3 **green onions, thinly sliced**

Prep: 20 minutes   Makes 4 servings

For dressing, in a food processor bowl or blender container combine ½ cup of the cashews, the water, garlic, salt, and onion powder. Cover and blend until mixture is smooth and creamy. (Mixture will thicken as it purees.) Stir in lemon juice.

In a salad bowl toss together the greens, tomatoes, peas, raisins, and green onions. To serve, divide among 4 serving plates. Sprinkle with remaining cashews. Drizzle dressing over each serving.

Nutrition facts per serving: 234 cal., 12 g total fat (2 g sat. fat), 0 mg chol., 304 mg sodium, 28 g carbo., 7 g fiber, 7 g pro. Daily values: 9% vit. A, 54% vit. C, 5% calcium, 19% iron

soba salad with
sesame-ginger dressing

All over Japan, at almost any hour, the national passion for noodles—including buckwheat soba—is fed by restaurants and street carts that serve nothing else. See why the locals line up for them daily.

Start to finish: 20 minutes   Makes 4 servings

For dressing, in a screw-top jar combine vinegar, water, cooking oil, sesame oil, ginger, and soy sauce. Cover and shake well. Set aside.

Meanwhile, cook soba noodles, uncovered, in a large pan of lightly salted boiling water about 3 minutes or until tender; drain. Rinse with cold water; drain well.

To serve, transfer cooked noodles to a large mixing bowl. Stir in the cucumber and carrot. Drizzle dressing over all; toss lightly to coat. Sprinkle with peanuts.

Nutrition facts per serving: 312 cal., 11 g total fat (2 g sat. fat), 0 mg chol., 597 mg sodium, 48 g carbo., 3 g fiber, 11 g pro. Daily values: 39% vit. A, 4% vit. C, 2% calcium, 13% iron

- 3 tablespoons white wine vinegar
- 1 tablespoon water
- 1 tablespoon cooking oil
- 1 teaspoon toasted sesame oil
- ½ teaspoon ground ginger
- ½ teaspoon soy sauce
- 8 ounces broken dried soba (buckwheat) noodles
- 1 cup chopped, seeded cucumber
- ½ cup shredded carrot
- ⅓ cup chopped peanuts

SO, what's soba?
Whether floating in a steaming bowl of soup or tossed in a chilled salad, brownish buckwheat soba noodles are a favorite Japanese fast food. Uncooked soba is sold in packages at Asian markets and most natural food stores, but in a pinch, you can substitute a narrow whole wheat ribbon pasta like linguine.

in the
soup

spring vegetable soup

This is one super meal-in-a-bowl. Served in hollowed loaves of bread, this elegant potage scores high points for presentation—just the ticket for a casual dinner get-together or family celebration.

Start to finish: 25 minutes   Makes 4 servings

In a medium saucepan combine 3 cups of the broth, the water chestnuts, pasta, and savory. Bring to boiling. Reduce heat and simmer, covered, for 5 minutes.

Meanwhile, in a small bowl stir together the remaining ½ cup broth and the cornstarch; add to saucepan. Stir in asparagus and peas. Cook and stir until thickened and bubbly. Cook and and stir for 2 minutes more or until vegetables are tender and pasta is tender but firm. Stir in the mint.

To serve, ladle soup into bread bowls or serve with French bread.

Nutrition facts per serving: 268 cal., 3 g total fat (0 g sat. fat), 0 mg chol., 1,203 mg sodium, 56 g carbo., 2 g fiber, 9 g pro. Daily values: 6% vit. A, 23% vit. C, 5% calcium, 23% iron

Note: To make bread bowls, hollow out small round loaves, leaving ½-inch-thick shells. If desired, brush the insides with 2 tablespoons melted butter or margarine. Bake in a 350° oven for 10 minutes or until lightly toasted.

- 2 14½-ounce cans (3½ cups) vegetable or chicken broth
- 1 8-ounce can water chestnuts, drained and coarsely chopped
- 2 ounces dried angel hair pasta, broken (about 1 cup)
- ½ teaspoon snipped fresh savory or thyme
- 2 tablespoons cornstarch
- 8 ounces asparagus spears, cut into 1-inch pieces
- ½ cup frozen peas
- 2 tablespoons snipped fresh mint
- 4 5-inch bread bowls* or sliced French bread

spicy quinoa chili

A nutritious grain gives chili hot-heads a healthy reason to get fired up. Rather than the usual beans, nutty quinoa (KEEN-wah) ties the ingredients all together for a chili with novel texture but the same ol' heat.

1 large onion, chopped

4 cloves garlic, minced

4 teaspoons hot pepper oil or olive oil

2 14½-ounce cans (3½ cups) vegetable or chicken broth

2 cups water

1 10-ounce can chopped tomatoes with green chili peppers, undrained

4 teaspoons ground cumin

2 teaspoons chili powder

1 teaspoon ground coriander

1 cup quinoa, rinsed and drained

4 plum tomatoes, chopped

Prep: 10 minutes   Cook: 20 minutes   Makes 4 servings

In a large saucepan cook onion and garlic in hot oil over medium-high heat until tender. Stir in broth, water, undrained canned tomatoes, cumin, chili powder, and coriander. Stir in quinoa.

Bring to boiling. Reduce heat and simmer, covered, about 20 minutes or until quinoa is tender. Remove from heat; stir in tomatoes.

Nutrition facts per serving: 127 cal., 3 g total fat (0 g sat. fat), 0 mg chol., 1,712 mg sodium, 32 g carbo., 5 g fiber, 3 g pro. Daily values: 77% vit. A, 331% vit. C, 2% calcium, 16% iron

root vegetable
& bean soup

Dig root vegetables? Then this bean soup is for you. The herb-seasoned broth is stocked with subterranean specialties—potatoes, parsnips, rutabaga, onion, and carrots—made succulent via roasting.

Start to finish: 40 minutes   Makes 4 servings

In a large roasting pan toss parsnips, potato, rutabaga, carrots, and onion with oil; sprinkle with salt. Spread the vegetables in a single layer in the roasting pan. Roast in a 450° oven for 15 to 20 minutes or until the vegetables start to brown.

Meanwhile, in a large saucepan bring broth and beans to boiling; add roasted vegetables. Return to boiling. Reduce heat and simmer, covered, about 5 minutes or until vegetables are tender. Stir in thyme. (For a thicker consistency, mash vegetables and beans slightly.)

Nutrition facts per serving: 274 cal., 5 g total fat (1 g sat. fat), 0 mg chol., 1,338 mg sodium, 58 g carbo., 13 g fiber, 11 g pro. Daily values: 150% vit. A, 44% vit. C, 8% calcium, 22% iron

salts of the earth
As a seasoning, salt reigns supreme. But you have other options beyond table salt. Sea salt, from sea water, is favored by professional chefs for its fresh, complex, marine flavor, and comes coarse for grinding or finely ground. Coarse-grained kosher salt is less salty tasting than either sea salt or table salt and has a rough texture.

- 2 medium parsnips, peeled and cut into ½-inch pieces (1½ cups)
- 1 medium potato, cut into ½-inch pieces (1 cup)
- 1 small rutabaga, peeled and cut into ½-inch pieces (1 cup)
- 2 medium carrots, sliced ½ inch thick (1 cup)
- 1 medium onion, cut into 8 wedges
- 1 tablespoon olive oil
- ½ teaspoon sea salt or kosher salt
- 3 cups vegetable or chicken broth
- 1 15-ounce can small red beans, garbanzo beans, or great Northern beans, rinsed and drained
- 2 teaspoons snipped fresh thyme

squash & papaya soup

Despite a demure demeanor, this golden fruit-and-vegetable soup is hot stuff. Giving it bold personality are nuances of Indian curry mixed with hints of garlic, ginger, and red pepper. Pour the soup over wheat berries for a satisfying meal.

2 cloves garlic, minced

1 tablespoon olive oil

1 teaspoon curry powder

½ teaspoon ground ginger

⅛ teaspoon ground red pepper (optional)

2 14½-ounce cans (3½ cups) vegetable or chicken broth

3 cups chopped, seeded, and peeled butternut squash

1 cup finely chopped papaya, peaches, or nectarines

2⅔ cups cooked wheat berries*

2 tablespoons snipped fresh cilantro (optional)

Prep: 25 minutes   Cook: 20 minutes   Makes 4 servings

In a large saucepan cook garlic in hot oil over medium heat for 30 seconds. Add curry powder, ginger, and, if desired, red pepper. Cook and stir 1 minute more. Stir in broth, squash, and papaya.

Bring mixture to boiling. Reduce heat and simmer, covered, about 20 minutes or until squash is tender. Cool slightly.

Place half of the squash mixture in a food processor bowl or blender container. Cover and process until smooth. Repeat with remaining squash mixture. Return processed mixture to saucepan and heat through. To serve, divide wheat berries among 4 soup bowls; add soup. If desired, sprinkle each serving with cilantro.

Nutrition facts per serving: 248 cal., 5 g total fat (1 g sat. fat), 0 mg chol., 823 mg sodium, 53 g carbo., 4 g fiber, 7 g pro. Daily values: 71% vit. A, 59% vit. C, 5% calcium, 21% iron

Note: To cook wheat berries, bring 3 cups water to boiling. Add 1 cup wheat berries. Return to boiling. Reduce heat and simmer, covered, about 1 hour or until tender. Drain well. If desired, cover and refrigerate for up to 3 days. Reheat before serving.

red sweet pepper soup

You'll appreciate the beauty of this rosy puree. It's created for convenience with instant couscous that gets plump and tender right in the hot soup—no precooking required. Prepared roasted sweet peppers shave time, but not taste.

½ cup chopped carrot

½ cup chopped celery

¼ cup chopped onion

4 cloves garlic, minced

1 teaspoon olive oil

4 14½-ounce cans (7 cups) vegetable or chicken broth

1 15-ounce jar roasted red sweet peppers

1 cup chopped potato

1 tablespoon snipped fresh oregano

1 teaspoon snipped fresh thyme

¼ cup quick-cooking couscous

Start to finish: 30 minutes   Makes 4 servings

In a Dutch oven cook carrot, celery, onion, and garlic in hot oil for 3 to 4 minutes or until tender. Stir in broth, roasted sweet peppers, and potato. Bring to boiling. Reduce heat and simmer, covered, for 15 minutes. Cool slightly. Stir in oregano and thyme.

Place one-third of the broth mixture in a food processor bowl or blender container. Cover and process until almost smooth. Repeat with remaining broth mixture.

Return soup to pan; stir in couscous. Cover and let stand for 5 minutes.

Nutrition facts per serving: 127 cal., 3 g total fat (0 g sat. fat), 0 mg chol., 1,712 mg sodium, 32 g carbo., 5 g fiber, 3 g pro. Daily values: 77% vit. A, 331% vit. C, 2% calcium, 16% iron

yellow split pea dhal

Try comfort food, Indian style. In Hindi, *dhal* refers to all split grains, legumes, and seeds—the major source of protein in the Indian diet. As further comfort, it's just as good when made ahead and briefly reheated.

Prep: 15 minutes   Cook: 45 minutes   Makes 4 servings

In a medium saucepan bring water and salt to boiling; add split peas. Return to boiling. Reduce heat and simmer, covered, about 45 minutes or until tender. Do not drain.

Meanwhile, place fresh vegetables in a steamer basket over boiling water; cover. Steam about 10 minutes or until crisp-tender; drain. Or, cook frozen vegetables according to package directions. Set vegetables aside.

In a small skillet cook curry powder, cumin, turmeric, ginger, and red pepper in hot oil for 1 to 2 minutes or until fragrant.

In a food processor bowl or blender container combine the undrained split peas and the spice mixture. Cover and process until combined. If too thick, add a little warm broth or water. Transfer split pea mixture to a medium saucepan. Stir in the steamed vegetables; heat through.

Nutrition facts per serving: 249 cal., 5 g total fat (1 g sat. fat), 0 mg chol., 317 mg sodium, 40 g carbo., 6 g fiber, 15 g pro. Daily values: 88% vit. A, 82% vit. C, 8% calcium, 27% iron

To make ahead: Prepare the soup up to 24 hours ahead. Cover and refrigerate. Reheat over medium heat, covered, about 10 minutes or until heated through.

- 4 cups water
- ½ teaspoon salt
- 1 cup dry yellow split peas, rinsed and drained
- 4 cups cut-up fresh vegetables, such as cauliflower, broccoli, green beans, or carrots, or one 16-ounce package loose-pack frozen vegetables
- 1 teaspoon curry powder
- 1 teaspoon ground cumin
- ¼ teaspoon turmeric
- ¼ teaspoon ground ginger
- ⅛ teaspoon ground red pepper
- 1 tablespoon olive oil

tomato &
wild mushroom soup

When foraging for the wild mushrooms that give this soup its woodsy depth of flavor, look no further than the produce section of your local supermarket. There you'll find a bounty of exotic types ready to be gathered.

1 medium onion, chopped

2 cloves garlic, minced

1 tablespoon olive oil

8 ounces fresh mushrooms, such as porcini, portobello, or button, coarsely chopped (3 cups)

1 pound plum tomatoes, chopped

3 cups vegetable or chicken broth

¼ cup finely shredded Romano or Parmesan cheese

¼ cup shredded fresh basil or 2 tablespoons snipped fresh thyme or marjoram

Start to finish: 30 minutes   Makes 3 servings

In a large saucepan cook onion and garlic in hot oil over medium heat until onion is tender. Add mushrooms; cook for 5 to 7 minutes more or until mushrooms are tender, stirring occasionally.

Add tomatoes and broth to mushroom mixture. Bring to boiling. Reduce heat and simmer, covered, for 10 minutes.

To serve, sprinkle with cheese and basil. If desired, season to taste with freshly ground pepper.

Nutrition facts per serving: 140 cal., 9 g total fat (1 g sat. fat), 7 mg chol., 1,049 mg sodium, 17 g carbo., 3 g fiber, 7 g pro. Daily values: 12% vit. A, 55% vit. C, 8% calcium, 15% iron

wild about mushrooms
If common button or other cultivated mushrooms bore you, take a walk on the wild side with fresh exotics such as fragrant Italian porcini, trumpetlike chanterelles, or meaty morels. Intensely flavored dried porcini and morel mushrooms are another option. To rehydrate, soak them in warm water for 30 minutes and drain well.

cucumber & mint soup

Feel a sudden drop in temperature? It's not the weather, but this refreshing, ice-cold puree inspired by Indian raitas. On a sultry day, it's like air-conditioning in a bowl.

Prep: 15 minutes   Freeze: 15 minutes   Makes 3 servings

Peel cucumbers; cut in half lengthwise. Scoop out seeds and discard. Cut the cucumbers into ½-inch-thick slices. (You should have 3 cups).

In a food processor bowl or blender container combine the cucumber, yogurt, lime juice, honey, cumin, and salt. Cover and process until smooth. If desired, stir in milk. Stir in mint. Cover and freeze for 15 minutes. (Or chill for up to 24 hours.) Stir before serving.

Nutrition facts per serving: 143 cal., 3 g total fat (2 g sat. fat), 9 mg chol., 290 mg sodium, 21 g carbo., 2 g fiber, 10 g pro. Daily values: 10% vit. A, 34% vit. C, 27% calcium, 18% iron

- 2 medium cucumbers
- 2 8-ounce cartons plain low-fat yogurt
- 2 tablespoons lime juice
- 2 teaspoons honey
- ½ teaspoon ground cumin
- ¼ teaspoon salt
- 2 tablespoons milk (optional)
- ⅓ cup snipped fresh mint

sandwich
savoir faire

sweet & spicy spring rolls

With coconut for sweet and fiery Japanese wasabi for spicy, these vegetable-packed rolls are a sense sensation. Wasabi, a sushi condiment, is a pungent green paste that tastes like horseradish. Find it, along with rice paper, with other Asian ingredients.

Start to finish: 25 minutes Makes 6 spring rolls

Carefully dip each rice paper quickly in water and place between paper towels or clean cotton dish towels. Let stand for 10 minutes.

Meanwhile, in a small bowl combine the ginger, wasabi paste, and lime juice. Stir in mayonnaise.

In a large mixing bowl toss together the shredded broccoli, tofu, and coconut. Add mayonnaise mixture; toss to coat.

Line each rice paper with a lettuce leaf. Spoon broccoli mixture over lettuce. Wrap rice paper around broccoli mixture. Serve with sauce.

Dipping Sauce: Stir together 1 tablespoon soy sauce, 1 tablespoon lime juice, and ¼ teaspoon crushed red pepper.

Nutrition facts per spring roll: 123 cal., 5 g total fat (1 g sat. fat), 0 mg chol., 318 mg sodium, 16 g carbo., 1 g fiber, 3 g pro. Daily values: 2% vit. A, 25% vit. C, 1% calcium, 5% iron

6 8-inch round rice papers

2 teaspoons grated fresh ginger

1 to 2 teaspoons wasabi paste

1 teaspoon lime juice

⅓ cup light mayonnaise dressing or salad dressing

2 cups packaged shredded broccoli (broccoli slaw mix)

½ of a 10½-ounce package extra-firm tofu (fresh bean curd), drained and finely chopped (1 cup)

¼ cup flaked coconut

6 romaine lettuce leaves

1 recipe Dipping Sauce

peppery artichoke pitas

Stuck in traffic? No time to shop? These pitas, filled with ingredients pulled mostly from the pantry—tender artichokes, cooked beans, and bottled garlic dressing—put a premium on convenience and a great dinner on the table.

1 **15-ounce can great Northern beans, rinsed and drained**

1 **13¾- to 14-ounce can artichoke hearts, drained and coarsely chopped**

½ **cup torn arugula or spinach**

¼ **cup bottled creamy garlic salad dressing**

¼ **teaspoon cracked black pepper**

3 **pita bread rounds, halved crosswise**

Start to finish: 20 minutes   Makes 6 servings

In a medium mixing bowl combine beans, artichoke hearts, arugula, salad dressing, and pepper. Spoon into pita bread halves to serve.

Nutrition facts per serving: 227 cal., 5 g total fat (1 g sat. fat), 3 mg chol., 269 mg sodium, 38 g carbo., 6 g fiber, 10 g pro. Daily values: 1% vit. A, 8% vit. C, 7% calcium, 16% iron

arugula (aka rocket or roquette)

Whatever you call it, arugula (ah-ROO-guh-lah) is a peppery salad green sometimes mistaken for dandelion. Mature leaves are large and very pungent—tasty accents to milder greens in a mixed salad. Less assertive young leaves can be used alone. Rinse leaves well in cold water, pat dry, and chill in a plastic bag for up to 2 days.

cucumber &
apricot sandwiches

Just a little bit retro is this hearty cucumber sandwich sweetened with thin slices of fresh fruit. But with ingredients like pungent basil, crunchy sprouts, and peppery arugula, it's up to the minute in taste and freshness.

85

Start to finish: 15 minutes   Makes 4 servings

Peel cucumber. Cut in half lengthwise and scoop out seeds. Thinly slice cucumber; set aside.

In a small bowl combine cream cheese, basil, and, if desired, salt. Spread about 1 tablespoon of the cheese mixture on one side of each bread slice. Top bread with cucumber slices, apricot slices, sprouts, and arugula. Top with remaining 4 bread slices. Cut each sandwich in half.

Serve sandwiches immediately or cover and chill for up to 2 hours.

Nutrition facts per serving: 238 cal., 10 g total fat (5 g sat. fat), 25 mg chol., 416 mg sodium, 31 g carbo., 3 g fiber, 9 g pro. Daily values: 12% vit. A, 6% vit. C, 6% calcium, 12% iron

1 **large cucumber**

½ **of an 8-ounce package reduced-fat cream cheese (Neufchâtel), softened**

2 **tablespoons snipped fresh basil**

⅛ **teaspoon salt (optional)**

8 **slices firm-textured whole wheat bread**

2 **large apricots or 1 nectarine, pitted and thinly sliced**

¼ **cup assorted fresh broccoli or radish sprouts**

¼ **cup arugula leaves or cilantro sprigs**

sautéed onion &
tomato sandwiches

When laps double as the dining table, the best TV dinner is something easy and out-of-hand. This hearty whole-grain sandwich serves perfectly. Pass around beer, brownies, and your biggest napkins.

86

2 medium onions, sliced

1 teaspoon olive oil

8 slices hearty whole grain bread
(toasted, if desired)

  Honey mustard

3 small red and/or yellow tomatoes,
thinly sliced

4 lettuce leaves, shredded

  Small basil leaves

4 ounces spreadable Brie cheese
or soft-style cream cheese

Start to finish: 20 minutes   Makes 4 servings

In a large skillet cook onion slices in hot oil over medium-high heat for 5 to 7 minutes or until tender and just starting to brown. Remove the skillet from heat; cool onions slightly.

To assemble, lightly spread one side of 4 bread slices with honey mustard. Top with onion slices, tomato slices, and lettuce. Sprinkle with basil. Spread one side of each of the 4 remaining bread slices with Brie cheese; place atop sandwiches, spread side down.

Nutrition facts per serving: 287 cal., 12 g total fat (6 g sat. fat), 28 mg chol., 490 mg sodium, 35 g carbo., 1 g fiber, 12 g pro. Daily values: 8% vit. A, 16% vit. C, 8% calcium, 15% iron

open-face portobello sandwiches

Turn a familiar hors d'oeuvre—bread-stuffed mushrooms—upside down for a new lease on life as a stunning open-face sandwich. Now it's bread on the bottom, mushrooms on top.

89

Prep: 25 minutes   Makes 4 servings

In a small mixing bowl combine tomato, basil, and salt; set aside. Clean mushrooms; cut off stems even with caps. Discard stems.

Combine vinegar and oil; gently brush over the mushrooms. Place mushrooms on the unheated rack of the broiler pan. Broil mushrooms 4 to 5 inches from the heat for 6 to 8 minutes or just until tender, turning once.* Drain mushrooms on paper towels. Thinly slice mushrooms.

Place bread on a baking sheet. Place under broiler for 2 to 3 minutes or until heated through.

To serve, top bread with mushroom slices and tomato mixture. If desired, top with Parmesan cheese.

Nutrition facts per serving: 161 cal., 3 g total fat (1 g sat. fat), 2 mg chol., 71 mg sodium, 29 g carbo., 3 g fiber, 7 g pro. Daily values: 1% vit. A, 15% vit. C, 4% calcium, 12% iron

Note: If desired, grill mushrooms on the rack of an uncovered grill directly over medium heat for 6 to 8 minutes or just until tender, turning once.

- 1 medium tomato, chopped (⅔ cup)
- 2 teaspoons snipped fresh basil, thyme, and/or oregano
- ⅛ teaspoon salt
- 2 medium fresh portobello mushrooms (about 4 inches in diameter)
- 1 teaspoon balsamic vinegar or red wine vinegar
- ½ teaspoon olive oil
- ½ of a 12-inch Italian flat bread (focaccia), quartered, or ½ of a 12-inch thin-crust Italian bread shell (Boboli)

  Finely shredded Parmesan cheese (optional)

tangy bean salad wraps

Using a variety of tortillas flavored with tomato-basil, pesto, fresh herb, or whole wheat makes this rapid wrap, stuffed with favorite Mexican ingredients, new every time you serve it.

4 8-inch flavored or plain flour tortillas

1 15-ounce can black beans, rinsed, drained, and slightly mashed

½ cup chopped green sweet pepper or 1 jalapeño pepper, seeded and finely chopped

2 tablespoons snipped fresh cilantro

⅓ cup light mayonnaise dressing or salad dressing

1 tablespoon lime juice

Leaf lettuce

Start to finish: 15 minutes   Makes 4 servings

Wrap the tortillas in foil. Heat in a 350° oven for 10 minutes to soften. (Or, wrap tortillas in microwave-safe paper towels. Microwave on high for 30 seconds.)

Meanwhile, in a medium bowl combine black beans, sweet pepper, and cilantro. Stir in light mayonnaise dressing and lime juice. To serve, spread mixture evenly over tortillas. Top with lettuce leaves. Roll up tortillas.

Nutrition facts per serving: 230 cal., 9 g total fat (2 g sat. fat), 0 mg chol., 531 mg sodium, 32 g carbo., 6 g fiber, 9 g pro. Daily values: 1% vit. A, 21% vit. C, 6% calcium, 14% iron

falafel-millet burgers with tomato relish

Meet the new meatless burger! It's a tasty take on falafel, a popular street snack from the Middle East, streamlined with a mix, then customized with crunchy millet and a juicy garden relish.

Start to finish: 30 minutes   Makes 6 servings

In a medium bowl combine falafel mix and millet; stir in water. Let stand at room temperature about 10 minutes or until water is absorbed. Shape falafel mixture into six ½-inch-thick patties.

Meanwhile, for tomato relish, in a medium bowl combine tomatoes, sweet pepper, green onions, pepper, and garlic. Set aside.

In a large skillet cook 3 of the patties, uncovered, in 1 tablespoon of the hot oil over medium-high heat for 3 minutes. Turn patties over and cook for 2 to 3 minutes more or until golden brown. Remove patties from skillet and keep warm. Repeat with remaining patties and oil.

To serve, place a patty on the bottom half of each bun. Using a slotted spoon, top each with some of the tomato relish. Add bun tops.

Nutrition facts per serving: 320 cal., 7 g total fat (1 g sat. fat), 0 mg chol., 979 mg sodium, 55 g carbo., 11 g fiber, 19 g pro. Daily values: 4% vit. A, 26% vit. C, 7% calcium, 23% iron

- 2 cups dry falafel mix
- ¼ cup millet
- 1⅓ cups cold water
- 2 medium tomatoes, seeded and chopped (1¼ cups)
- 1 small green sweet pepper, chopped (½ cup)
- 4 green onions, thinly sliced
- ¼ teaspoon pepper
- 1 clove garlic, minced
- 2 tablespoons olive oil
- 6 whole grain hamburger buns, split and toasted

grilled eggplant &
sweet pepper sandwiches

Grills fire up when hot summer days shut down kitchens, and simple feasts—such as this Mediterranean stack of smoky eggplant and sweet peppers anchored with a smear of tangy goat cheese—are the rule.

- **2 medium green, red, and/or yellow sweet peppers**
- **1 small eggplant (about 12 ounces), cut into 12 slices**
- **1 tablespoon olive oil**
- **8 ½-inch-thick slices French bread**
- **4 ounces soft goat cheese (chèvre)**
- **¼ cup Dijon-style mustard**

Start to finish: 25 minutes   Makes 4 servings

Quarter the sweet peppers lengthwise; remove and discard the stems, seeds, and membranes.

Brush eggplant slices with oil. Grill eggplant slices and sweet pepper quarters on the rack of an uncovered grill directly over medium-hot coals for 4 minutes. Turn and grill 3 to 5 minutes more or until eggplant is tender and sweet peppers are slightly charred. Remove vegetables from grill; set aside.

Spread 1 side of each French bread slice with goat cheese and mustard. Layer 3 eggplant slices and 2 sweet pepper quarters on 4 of the bread slices. Top with remaining bread slices. Serve warm.

Nutrition facts per serving: 240 cal., 13 g total fat (5 g sat. fat), 25 mg chol., 698 mg sodium, 21 g carbo., 2 g fiber, 9 g pro. Daily values: 6% vit. A, 46% vit. C, 4% calcium, 8% iron

95

METRIC COOKING HINTS

By making a few conversions, cooks in Australia, Canada, and the United Kingdom can use the recipes in *Better Homes and Gardens® Fresh and Simple™ Vegetable Dinners* with confidence. The charts on this page provide a guide for converting measurements from the U.S. customary system, which is used throughout this book, to the imperial and metric systems. There also is a conversion table for oven temperatures to accommodate the differences in oven calibrations.

Product Differences: Most of the ingredients called for in the recipes in this book are available in English-speaking countries. However, some are known by different names. Here are some common American ingredients and their possible counterparts:

- Sugar is granulated or castor sugar.
- Powdered sugar is icing sugar.
- All-purpose flour is plain household flour or white flour. When self-rising flour is used in place of all-purpose flour in a recipe that calls for leavening, omit the leavening agent (baking soda or baking powder) and salt.
- Light-colored corn syrup is golden syrup.
- Cornstarch is cornflour.
- Baking soda is bicarbonate of soda.
- Vanilla is vanilla essence.
- Green, red, or yellow sweet peppers are capsicums.
- Golden raisins are sultanas.

Volume and Weight: Americans traditionally use cup measures for liquid and solid ingredients. The chart, above right, shows the approximate imperial and metric equivalents. If you are accustomed to weighing solid ingredients, the following approximate equivalents will be helpful.

- 1 cup butter, castor sugar, or rice = 8 ounces = about 250 grams
- 1 cup flour = 4 ounces = about 125 grams
- 1 cup icing sugar = 5 ounces = about 150 grams

Spoon measures are used for smaller amounts of ingredients. Although the size of the tablespoon varies slightly in different countries, for practical purposes and for recipes in this book, a straight substitution is all that's necessary.

Measurements made using cups or spoons always should be level unless stated otherwise.

Equivalents: U.S. = Australia/U.K.

⅛ teaspoon = 0.5 ml
¼ teaspoon = 1 ml
½ teaspoon = 2 ml
1 teaspoon = 5 ml
1 tablespoon = 1 tablespoon
¼ cup = 2 tablespoons = 2 fluid ounces = 60 ml
⅓ cup = ¼ cup = 3 fluid ounces = 90 ml
½ cup = ⅓ cup = 4 fluid ounces = 120 ml
⅔ cup = ½ cup = 5 fluid ounces = 150 ml
¾ cup = ⅔ cup = 6 fluid ounces = 180 ml
1 cup = ¾ cup = 8 fluid ounces = 240 ml
1¼ cups = 1 cup
2 cups = 1 pint
1 quart = 1 liter
½ inch = 1.27 cm
1 inch = 2.54 cm

Baking Pan Sizes

American	Metric
8×1½-inch round baking pan	20×4-cm cake tin
9×1½-inch round baking pan	23×3.5-cm cake tin
11×7×1½-inch baking pan	28×18×4-cm baking tin
13×9×2-inch baking pan	30×20×3-cm baking tin
2-quart rectangular baking dish	30×20×3-cm baking tin
15×10×1-inch baking pan	30×25×2-cm baking tin (Swiss roll tin)
9-inch pie plate	22×4- or 23×4-cm pie plate
7- or 8-inch springform pan	18- or 20-cm springform or loose-bottom cake tin
9×5×3-inch loaf pan	23×13×7-cm or 2-pound narrow loaf tin or pâté tin
1½-quart casserole	1.5-liter casserole
2-quart casserole	2-liter casserole

Oven Temperature Equivalents

Fahrenheit Setting	Celsius Setting*	Gas Setting
300°F	150°C	Gas Mark 2 (slow)
325°F	160°C	Gas Mark 3 (moderately slow)
350°F	180°C	Gas Mark 4 (moderate)
375°F	190°C	Gas Mark 5 (moderately hot)
400°F	200°C	Gas Mark 6 (hot)
425°F	220°C	Gas Mark 7
450°F	230°C	Gas Mark 8 (very hot)
Broil		Grill

Electric and gas ovens may be calibrated using Celsius. However, for an electric oven, increase the Celsius setting 10 to 20 degrees when cooking above 160°C. For convection or forced-air ovens (gas or electric), lower the temperature setting 10°C when cooking at all heat levels.